Monographic Journals of the Near East   *Afroasiatic Linguistics* 6/5 (August 1979)

T0153714

GRAMMATICAL CATEGORIES OF VERB STEMS AND THE MARKING OF MOOD, AKTIONSART, AND ASPECT IN CHADIC*

by

Ekkehard Wolff
University of Hamburg

Current theories on the nature and history of the Chadic verbal system claim that Proto-Chadic had (a) a fundamental binary distinction of aspect, in which (b) the Perfective was the unmarked category, and that (c) a characteristically marked Imperfective verb stem can be reconstructed for the proto-language. This paper presents comparative evidence from 10 languages of the Biu-Mandara branch of Chadic, on the basis of which all three claims are rejected. The existence of dichotomous aspect systems in some modern Chadic languages is explained by and related to essentially three simplification and/or elaboration processes which are attributed to the linguistic history of the individual branches of the family: (1) loss of stem-final marking devices with compensatory shift to preverbal marking, (2) redesignation of the proto-verbal noun, and (3) redesignation of verbal plurals.

TABLE OF CONTENTS

*This is a much revised version of a paper which was distributed to participants of the 8th Conference on African Linguistics, April 1-3, 1977, at UCLA. I am indebted to Paul Newman, Leiden, for a most stimulating discussion of an earlier version of this paper.

1. INTRODUCTION

1.1 GENERAL PRELIMINARIES

One of the major points in the present discussion among Chadicists is the question of whi
properties can be attributed to the Proto-Chadic (PC) verbal system. For more than a
decade now we have been told that there was, first of all, a fundamental binary distincti
of "aspect". In this dichotomous system the Imperfective is viewed as the marked counter
part of the unmarked Perfective. These aspects are used to classify the various "tenses"
at a higher level of analysis. (This is basically the theory which H. Jungraithmayr has
developed in various publications since 1966. He views the postulated aspectual dichotom
as a retention from Proto-Afroasiatic (P-AA).) We have been told further that PC verbs
could be classified according to final vowel and tone (Newman 1975). That this lexical
stem vowel distinction appeared only in the "Perfective" but was neutralized in the
"Subjunctive" stem was one of the contributions of Schuh (1976). Further, PC must have
known a "gerundive" (Newman and Schuh 1974) or, as it is also called a "true (or primary)
verbal noun" (Schuh 1976). Further, we have been told that PC knew plural verb stems whi
were independent of the mood-, aktionsart-, or aspect-specified formations in which they
occurred (Wolff 1977b). All seem to agree that there was at least one—if not more
(Newman and Schuh 1974)—set(s) of preverbal pronouns to mark the subject. Between these

and the verb stem, particles could be inserted to mark the categories of mood, aktionsart, and aspect, henceforth jointly referred to as AUX-categories (Jungraithmayr (1966) and (in press b), Newman and Schuh (1974)—questioned again by Schuh (1976).

The most controversial issue seems to be the question of how the Imperfective (IPF) verb stem was formed in PC. Jungraithmayr (since 1968) has postulated a morphologically "extended" stem—at least in what he refers to as early stages of the development of Chadic languages (cf. section 3)—marked by "internal -a- and/or -a suffix" (collectively referred to as "apophony" by him in later works). By and large this was accepted in Newman and Schuh" (1974). In this respect, Schuh (1976:13) is in full agreement with Jungraith-mayr, assuming "a vowel -a- infixed within and/or suffixed to the verb root." Newman (1977a) accepts the existence of a PC Imperfective stem only cum grano salis. He definitely rejects the idea that apophony played any role in its formation. In Wolff (1977b) the hypothesis is advanced that IPF stems in modern Chadic languages, when they are marked in a specific way, i.e. by consonant gemination and/or vowel alternations, might have developed from verbal plurals. All accept, basically, Jungraithmayr's claim "that even though all Chadic languages have more than two or three verb aspects/tenses/moods, some of these are demon-strably derivable from other, more basic ones" as Schuh (1976:7) put it.

The discussion has reached a point where we ought to stop and ask ourselves a few basic questions in order to clarify again what we are actually reasoning about:

(1) What exactly do we mean by "aspect" in the context of Chadic language study?

(2) Did Proto-Chadic necessarily have a dichotomous aspect system based on the unmarked/ marked opposition of Perfective/Imperfective, or could the verbal systems of modern Chadic languages be traced back to another type of (proto-)system?

(3) If it does not turn out to be necessary to postulate an aspect system of the type outlined, how can the existence of binary aspect systems in modern Chadic languages be explained?

(4) Whatever the system of the proto-language was, what was marked and how was it marked?

This paper attempts to give answers to these questions. Most of all I intend to show that to reconstruct an Imperfective stem for Proto-Chadic is not the only possibility to explain the development of modern Chadic verbal systems. Contrary to current theories held about the nature and history of the Chadic verbal system I shall propose that the development of marked verb aspects—Imperfective and Perfective—is innovative rather than archaic in Chadic. This rather radical departure from traditional concepts held about the Chadic verbal system rests upon a number of observations, hypotheses, and assumptions, which again are based on the comparative analysis of the verbal systems of 10 Biu-Mandara languages plus a critical evaluation of the relevant works of Jungraithmayr, Newman, and Schuh. I have added my own interpretation of observations concerning the affinity of verbal plurality, iterative and durative aktionsarten, and imperfective aspect in a number of non-Biu-Mandara languages of Chadic.

Until today, the discussion of properties of the PC verbal system has suffered from the neglect of evidence from the languages of the Biu-Mandara branch of the family, although in one of his latest and clearest contributions on the matter, Jungraithmayr (in press b) included a discussion of four Biu-Mandara (BM) languages, Gisiga, Musgu, Masa, and Zime, of which two (Masa, Zime) may not even belong to this branch (cf. Newman (1977b)). However, it becomes obvious by HJ's own descriptions that these languages are not very well suited to prove his particular theory. According to Jungraithmayr (but cf. 2.2.1.8 and 2.2.2 below) Gisiga has given up aspectual differentiation of verb stems (HJ: "stage IV—no changes"), the other three are said to "have acquired a new method of alternation, namely TONAL mutation." Another major aim of this paper, beside presenting an alternative theory of the

historical development of the marking of mood, aspect, and aktionsart in Chadic, is
therefore to introduce comparative data from Biu-Mandara into the ongoing discussion.

Section 1.2 of the introduction discusses the term "aspect" as it is, was, and ought to be
applied in Chadic linguistics. Section 1.3 introduces hypotheses concerning the affinity
of verbal plurality, certain aktionsarten, and imperfectivity and directs attention to
related questions in comparative Semitic scholarship. Section 1.4 takes issue with the
postulate of a dichotomy of aspect in Chadic and how it was elaborated in a number of
important contributions by Jungraithmayr.

Section 2.1 contains my interpretation of what Newman and Schuh (1974) and Schuh (1976)
have so far established for Proto-West-Chadic. Section 2.2 outlines what can be reconstruc-
ed for Proto-Biu-Mandara and thus constitutes the main part of the paper. Section 2.3
attempts to filter out what we may assume for Proto-Chadic and how the proto-systems of
the different branches of Chadic might have developed from the reconstructed PC system.

Section 3 consists of a short summary and concluding remarks on the validity of Jungraithmayr's "Tentative four stage model for the development of the Chadic languages".

There remains one fact which deserves to be strongly emphasized: without the comparative
works of outstanding scholars in the Chadic field such as Jungraithmayr, Newman, and
Schuh, this presentation which in parts rests heavily on a synopsis of their ideas, would
have been impossible.

1.2 THE TERM "ASPECT" IN THE CONTEXT OF CHADIC LANGUAGE STUDY

Before we continue to discuss the categories of mood, aspect, and aktionsart in Chadic, we
ought to establish what we mean by these terms.

For the purpose of this paper, "mood" is used to describe the distinction between Subjunctive
(SBJ) which is considered to be marked (at least semantically), and its unmarked opposition
which we might call Indicative. Indicative in this sense means nothing more than non-SBJ.
Within the subjunctive mood, we may distinguish between imperatives on the one hand and
paradigmatic sets such as jussives/optatives/subjunctives on the other hand, whatever the
terms are which are used in the descriptions of the individual languages.

As regards the discussion of the terms "aspect" and "aktionsart", we could start by
quoting from Comrie (1976:6f):

> "In addition to the term 'aspect', some linguists also make use of the
> term 'aktionsart' (plural: aktionsarten): this is a German word meaning
> 'kinds of action', and although there have been numerous attempts to coin
> an English equivalent, none of these has become generally accepted. The
> distinction is ... between aspect as a grammaticalization of the relevant
> semantic distinction, and aktionsart as a lexicalization of the distinc-
> tion provided that the lexicalization is by means of derivational morphol-
> ogy."

In African linguistics, the term "aspect" is quite often used in this sense of aktionsart an
may even include mood (as in Hausa scholarship). Sometimes "tense" is reserved for the
category of time reference (T), i.e. tempus (this only if any distinction is attempted at
all). It is typical of the best part of Chadic language descriptions that no distinction
is attempted, the main reason being that we lack a theory to help us analyze and understand
the rather complex systems of modern Chadic languages. Prolegomena to such a theory are
presented in this paper.

Writing in 1974, Jungraithmayr (in press b) tried to stop this confusing practice in the field of comparative Chadic verb morphology by attempting a hierarchical definition of "aspect" and "tense":

> "The verbal system of any given Chadic language consists of a number of conjugational forms which are usually called 'tenses' or 'aspects'. In this paper these two terms will be used differently. 'Tense' will continue to denote any verbal paradigmatic set (...), 'aspect', however, shall be reserved for the basic binary distinction between 'perfective' and 'imperfective'. For instance, conjugational forms like 'Perfect', 'Aorist', 'Narrative' are tenses based on the perfective aspect (stem), whereas 'Progressive', 'Future', 'Habitual' generally belong to the imperfective aspect base. It is superfluous to state that there can never be more than two aspects in the frame of such a concept ....
>
> "Compared with the perfective aspect form the imperfective aspect form is, in general, marked; in other words, the ipf. asp. form appears as an extension of the pf. asp. base."[1]

Jungraithmayr does not, however, distinguish aktionsarten from tempora in what he continues to call "tenses"; yet this had been already thought of as being important for Hausa, for instance, in the opinion of Klingenheben (1928/29), who distinguished mood, aktionsart, and tempus within the AUX-system of this language. For practical purposes it may also be advisable to single out a category Sequential (SQT) which is quite widespread in Chadic, relating one action to a foregoing or following one.

Jungraithmayr's suggestion is useful in that it relates the semantic content of aspect to recurring morphological features in the verb itself. The terms marked/unmarked are applied by Jungraithmayr as it seems to both morphological structure and general semantic notions. Giving priority to the semantics of a form, as HJ does in his later publications, one of the shortcomings of his approach turns out to be the fact that he allows the notion of markedness to be applied too extensively, including all kinds of phonological, morphological, and syntactical features.

For further usage of the term aspect in Chadic linguistics it is important to define what exactly we want it to denote. Rather than following usages of the term in established philologies with long terminological traditions (such as Greek, Slavonic, or Semitic scholarship) we shall follow a language independent approach as the one suggested by Comrie (1976) for defining "aspect", "perfectivity", and "imperfectivity".

ASPECT

> "Aspects are different ways of viewing the internal temporal constituency of a situation." (p. 3)

> "Aspect is not concerned with relating the time of the situation to any other time-point, but rather with the internal temporal constituency of the one situation; one could state the difference as one between situation-internal time (aspect) and situation-external time (tense)." (p. 5)

---

[1]The terms "stem" and "base" in the context of aspect formation seem to be used interchangeably by Jungraithmayr for reasons of stylistic variation only. They are not well-defined terms of his theory. For a theoretical model based on a strict analytical distinction of root/base/stem, cf. Wolff (1977b).

10

"Aspect as a grammatical category, just like any other grammatical category,
may be expressed by means of the inflectional morphology of the language
in question ...; it may also be expressed by means of periphrasis." (p. 9)

The definition of aspect by Comrie does not differentiate between aspect and aktionsart as
we shall propose to do for Chadic linguistics; it just sets apart from both aspect and
aktionsart what we call Time Reference (tempus).

There is no reason why we should not use established terms for the different aspects as
long as they serve our needs. "Perfective" and "Imperfective" are the terms best known
and usually used to describe binary aspect systems. "Aorist" is the term added for the
Greek three-term system which according to Lyons (1968:314) may well have been a feature
of the Indo-European parent-language. For reasons that have to do with the differentiation
of aspect and aktionsart in this paper, I shall use the term "Grundaspekt" (introduced by
Jungraithmayr (1966)) instead of aorist in a three-term aspect system. ("Aorist" will be
used for labelling the Grundaspekt's manifestation as aktionsart on a different level of
analysis.)

For Chadic, a three-term frame rather than a binary one must be applied to describe aspect
systems in modern languages of this family from a comparative point of view, in which
Perfective and Imperfective are both marked in relation to the Grundaspekt. Again we
follow Comrie (1976) as regards definitions:

GRUNDASPEKT

"Being the unmarked category in the system, its meaning can encompass that
of its marked counterpart(s). The clearest example of this situation is
where overt expression of the meaning of the marked category is always
optional, i.e. where the unmarked category can always be used, even in a
situation where the marked category would also be appropriate." (p. 112)

PERFECTIVE

"Perfectivity indicates the view of a situation as a single whole, without
distinction of the various separate phases that make up that situation."
(p. 16)

"It involves lack of explicit reference to the internal temporal constituency
of a situation, rather than explicitly implying the lack of such internal
temporal constituency." (p. 21)

IMPERFECTIVE

"The imperfective pays essential attention to the internal structure of the
situation." (p. 16)

"In involves the explicit reference to the internal temporal structure
of a situation, viewing a situation from within." (p. 24)

"Imperfectivity is not incompatible with perfectivity." (p. 24)

"Habitual and Continuous (Durative) are the most typical subdivisions of
imperfectivity." (p. 25)

The model suggested for modern Chadic language analysis in terms of aspect can thus be
graphically represented as follows, < + > indicating markedness, < - > representing
unmarked:

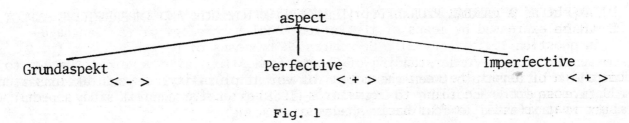

Fig. 1

In this model, the three-term opposition of perfective, imperfective, and grundaspekt encompasses two binary distinctions: perfective vs. non-perfective, and imperfective vs. non-imperfective.

It may turn out that the majority of modern Chadic languages can be described in terms of a binary aspect system, either Grundaspekt/Imperfective or Grundaspekt/Perfective. There is, however, at least one language in Chadic (Lamang = Biu-Mandara branch) in which a fully developed three-term aspect system Grundaspekt/Perfective/Imperfective operates the verbal system. Some languages of the family may even turn out to grammaticalize no aspectual distinctions at all.

In those modern Chadic languages which can be said to grammaticalize aspectual distinctions, one or more conjugational forms of the verb can be said to belong to one or the other aspect if we can establish that two or more of these forms share semantic as well as morphological features. This is apparent, for instance, in the choice of verb stems to which additional markers are preposed. These conjugational forms which can be classified according to which aspect they belong to, shall be henceforth referred to as "aktionsarten". In terms of discovery procedure we shall therefore approach the verbal system of a given Chadic language first of all by listing the various conjugational forms of verbs as the aktionsarten of this particular language. In a second step, we check whether certain aktionsarten can be classified together according to recurring morphological and semantic features relating to aspectual distinctions, thereby setting up aspectually identified sets of aktionsarten. In a third step, we check whether these aspectual distinctions apply to both the Indicative and the Subjunctive moods after we have previously established that modal distinctions are grammaticalized as well in the language under consideration. For these procedures we rely on a "maximal model" of mood, aspect, and aktionsart distinctions (AUX) which may be graphically represented as follows:

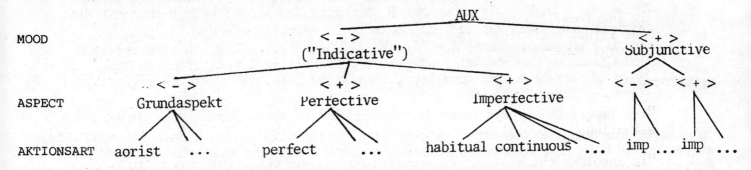

Fig. 2

The categories of Time Reference (T = tempus) and Sequential (SQT) which may also have been properties of the Proto-Chadic verbal system, shall not be discussed in any detail in this paper. (They must probably be considered to rank below aktionsart in our hierarchical model based on semantic features.)

1.3 THE AFFINITY OF VERBAL PLURALITY, ITERATIVE AKTIONSART, AND IMPERFECTIVE ASPECT IN CHADIC

It is essential for the understanding of Chadic (and Afroasiatic?) verbal systems to realize the relationship between the notion of verbal plurality, certain aktionsarten, and imperfective aspect. According to Dressler's (1968) extensive general study, verbal plurality is manifested in four basic shades of meaning:

(i)   distributive — in agreement to plurality of subject, object, or location of action;

(ii)   iterative   — in agreement to plurality of the action itself, i.e. its usage as frequentative, repetitive, etc. aktionsarten;

(iii) durative   — in agreement to the temporal extension of the action, i.e. its usage as continuous, habitual, etc. aktionsart;

(iv)   intensive

Dressler's analysis shows how verbal plurality may enter the AUX-system of a given language or language group: through its iterative and/or durative manifestations. Given the classification of aktionsarten into aspectual categories, imperfectivity as the common semantic denominator of iterative and durative aktionsarten becomes related to verbal plurality. Not only via aktionsarten and their aspectual properties can the affinity of imperfective and plurality be made plausible: there is a way in which to relate aspect and "quantity" in a straightforward manner:

> "Dieser Gegensatz 'ganzheitlich :: nicht-ganzheitlich' trifft das Wesen des Verbalaspekts jedenfalls besser als etwa das aus der Vermischung mit den Aktionsarten entstandene Begriffspaar 'punktuell :: linear (durativ)' oder der auf die griech.Grammatiker zurückgehende Begriff der Vollendetheit.

> "Zwei weiteren Erscheinungen wird das Konzept der Komplexivität gerecht, das des Zeitrichtungsbezugs nicht: 1. der Aspektkonkurrenz beim Imperativ, 2. der Bevorzugung des ipfv. Aspekts in negierten Sätzen.

> "Damit verwandt ist die 'quantitative' Auffassung des Verbalaspekts durch G. Devoto. Unabhängig davon hat F. Rundgren den Aspekt beim Verbum mit den Numerus beim Nomen verglichen: beim ipfv. Aspekt werde der Verbalinhalt analysiert, d.h. 'gezählt', beim pfv. nicht. Die betreffende Verbalquantität werde 'als integrale, intransitive Totalität angeschaut' (= pfv.)oder 'als eine summative, transitive Totalität wirklich erlebt'."
> (Dressler 1968:43)

In a paper presented to the first international Colloquium on the Chadic Language Family at Leiden in 1976, I attempted to relate the scattered evidence of characteristically marked "imperfective" verb stems (as labelled by Jungraithmayr) to the formation of verb plurals in Chadic (Wolff 1977b). It was shown that consonant reduplication and/or in-fixation of -a- are plural markers in the nominal as well as the verbal system and that they are of very great age in the family, if not in the Afroasiatic phylum as a whole. According to the data presented by Jungraithmayr in various publications, exactly these formatives are also used to mark "imperfective" verb stems in some Chadic languages, e.g. the Ron languages in West Chadic, Migama and others in East Chadic. A closer look reveals that in those cases, where imperfective aspect is marked "internally", plural formation and this marked aspect formation are incompatible: the non-plural/plural distinction within the verb is neutralized in the imperfective. I concluded that in the verbal system as a marked category "plurality" ought to be attributed historical priority over "aspectuality". It was suggested that verb plurals were originally marked by emination or reduplication of the final radical and/or vowel alternations (probable rigin: insertion of -*a*-) and eventually transformed into an aspect stem which indicated requentative/repetitive/habitual/etc. performance of action, i.e. Jungraithmayr's imperfective" verb stem. This development, however, i.e. the incorporation of verbal lurals into the inflexional AUX-system, was obviously restricted to a certain group of C dialects only.

hadic languages do not seem to be the only ones in which such a development could occur: he relationship between the (verb) stem with geminated second radical, traditionally held o mark "intensity" (but cf. Ryder (1974) for a different analysis), and a possible econd prefix conjugation of the type **yi-qabbar* (cf. Akkadian *iqabbar* "present tense"). eside the **yi-qbur* type is still a mystery for Semitic scholars, as it seems:

> "To postulate the existence of only one prefix-conjugation in Proto-Semitic is considered by some scholars an inadequate solution—nor does its indeterminate character as regards tense commend itself to them .... Mention has already been made of the hypothesis claiming a secondary origin of the Akkadian form *iqabbar* by means of a redesignation of the stem with geminated second radical, but the view has also been advanced that *iqabbar* was dropped or restricted in use in West Semitic on account of its formal identity with the imperfect of the geminated stem." (Moscati et al. 1969:134).

he general Afroasiatic nature of the problem becomes apparent when we look at the other anguage families within the phylum. Without entering into a detailed discussion at this occasion, we might quote just one sentence from Zaborski's (1975) study:

> "Although most if not all of the Cushitic languages have a frequentative-durative class of derived verbs with gemination (or partial reduplication), nevertheless it is dubious whether this class was used for the renewal of the Present (like in Proto-Semitic and in Berber) in Proto-Cushitic."
> (p. 165)

If we insist, however, at this premature stage, on advancing at least a working hypothesis to account for the general Afroasiatic picture, we could very tentatively assume that the Proto-Afroasiatic dialect cluster shared a "drift" towards integrating verbal plurals, which all of the dialects seem to have possessed, into their AUX-systems—based on the fact, that verbal plurals when they are used to indicate frequentative/repetitive/ habitual action have strong imperfective connotations ("Iterativity").

1.4 THE DEVELOPMENT OF THE POSTULATE OF A FUNDAMENTAL BINARY DISTINCTION OF ASPECT
     IN CHADIC

In a series of publications since 1966, Jungraithmayr[2] elaborated the theory of a "funda-mental binary distinction of aspect" in Chadic. According to him, the IPF is the marked counterpart of the (unmarked) PRF. This view of Chadic verbal systems was by and large accepted in subsequent comparative works on Chadic verbs, e.g. Newman and Schuh (1974), Schuh (1976), Wolff (1977b), and remained unchallenged until very recently, e.g. Newman (1977a). The wealth of Jungraithmayr's publications on the subject makes it necessary to outline the most important steps in the development of his ideas.

In a first step (1966), aspect and aktionsart were not explicitly distinguished. Morpho-logical similarity was given superior relevance over synchronic semantic content of a

---

[2]I am indebted to Prof. Jungraithmayr for permission to quote from unpublished papers.

given form. Limited to West-Chadic languages, the 1966 model can be extrapolated as (using the original labels):

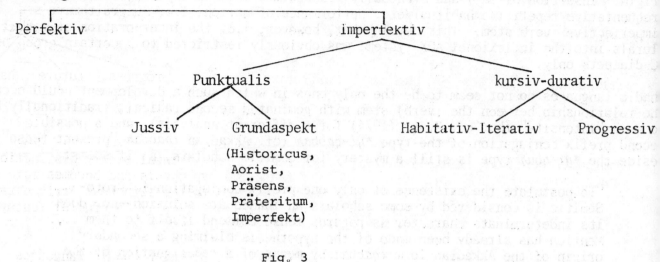

Fig. 3

The criteria were the morphological and syntactical structure of the finite verb forms:

"Perfektiv" = Subj.Pron.($\pm$Asp.Marker$_1$)+Verb Stem+Asp.Marker$_2$

"Punktualis" = Subj.Pron.+Verb Stem

"Progressiv" = Subj.Pron.+Asp.Marker+Nominal Stem

"Habitativ"(Ron languages only) = Infix -a(a)-

The relevance of such structural features is beyond doubt and, in my opinion, the 1966 publication is one of the most relevant in the field of comparative Chadic verb morphology. Yet, Jungraithmayr's interpretation of the data at the time and the model which he was deducing from it, could not be maintained, as he himself realized soon after, since it contained a confusion between Perfective aspect and Perfect aktionsart (explicitly so stated in a paper presented in 1970, published with unfortunate delay five years later (1975a:402)). In all later works the model was reduced to a simple dichotomy, now generally omitting the jussive/subjunctive from further consideration. In Jungraithmayr (1968a) it was, for instance, the following dichotomy:

"basic tense" vs. "present-habitative" (Ron)

"preterite" vs. "present" (Mubi)

In another publication of the same year, he distinguished for the Ron languages

(a) "basic (or short) form" vs. (b) "extended (or long) form"

which at the semantic level corresponded to

(a) "aorist or perfective 'Punktualis'" vs.

(b) "imperfective habitual (and/or progressive)".

A paper presented in 1974 (in press b) contains Jungraithmayr's clearest account of his theory. It is from now on based on the strict distinction of "aspect" and "tense" (cf. the quotation in 1.2 of this paper). From his 1974 presentation we can extrapolate the following graphic representation and compare it with the 1966 model. (Note his omission of the jussive/subjunctive from the "binary" system.)

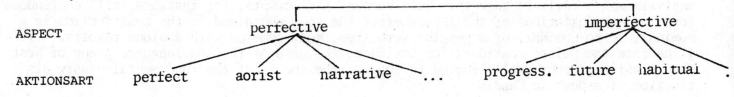

Fig. 4

From publication to publication the postulate of the fundamental binary distinction of aspect looses more and more its status as a tentative hypothesis and becomes more and more an established fact, so that in a paper presented to the 12th West African Languages Congress in 1976, Jungraithmayr could "characterize and exemplify a crucial feature of the verbal morphology of Chadic languages" by grossly simplifying that

> "Essentially, there are only two techniques by which Chadic languages
> mark the distinction between complete and incomplete action (Perfective/
> Imperfective, accompli/inaccompli, aorist /durative, extratemporal Present/
> Continuous etc.)—a distinction which seems to be basic to all verbal
> systems of Chadic languages. These techniques are 1) vowel change
> (apophony, ablaut) and 2) tone change ("abton") ...."

That "there is absolutely no evidence to support the idea that apophony played a role in the formation of the imperfective aspect stem in Proto-Chadic or in any early period in Chadic linguistic history" has been the point which Newman (1977a) tried to drive home in his recent criticism of Jungraithmayr's theory. Another shortcoming in the development of the theory is the occasional confusion of two discrete levels of analysis:

(i)   the *semantics* of the postulated aspectual dichotomy,

(ii) the *grammatical* level of the resp. morphological/syntactical manifestations.

This at times results in the almost arbitrary evaluation of verbal nouns as imperfective aspect stems in a number of languages which are cited to support the theory. Whether from a universal semantic point of view one could argue that the notions of continuousness, habituality, futurity, et al. necessarily imply a more general notion of "imperfectivity" and that therefore any language which grammaticalizes at least one of these notions automatically can be said to have a dichotomy of aspect in terms of perfectivity, is a question which we shall not pursue any further at this point. But unless the feature <+ipf> can be matched with a recurrent morphological feature or set of features in the verb stems of a given language or language group, a dichotomy of aspect in such universal semantic terms can play no role in the establishment of "grammatical relationship" for purposes of genetic classification of languages or language groups. Yet, this is exactly the goal which Jungraithmayr attempts to achieve.[3] Since, furthermore, it seems safe to assume the

---

[3]"For most of [the Chadic] languages basic LEXICAL information is available; reliable GRAMMATICAL data, however, is still scarce. Roughly speaking, grammatical documentation is sufficient to render possible some basic comparative work for about only one quarter of the languages, for example on verb morphology. Thus the classification of these languages as a "family" has so far to be based almost exclusively on lexical criteria, not on established grammatical relationship (cf. Newman-Ma 1966)." (Jungraithmayr, in press [b]: §1)

existence of some kind of verbal noun for the proto-language (because at least one kind
of nominalized verb stem seems to exist in every modern Chadic language) any comparative
analysis which fails to take this into account and accepts, for instance, all "continuous"
forms as manifestations of the IPF, whether the stem contained in the construction is a
nominal, verbo-nominal, or a genuine verb stem, must come up with dubious results.[4] To
illustrate the point, consider, for instance, the case of the Ron language group of West
Chadic which is continually quoted to support the theory of the fundamental binary distinction of aspect in Chadic.

It is obvious from the descriptions by Jungraithmayr (1970) that the "verbal noun" in the
Ron group of languages is formed on the basis of the "aspect I" stem, i.e. the non-imperfective aspect stem, since none of the characteristic morphological features of the
"aspect II" stem, i.e. "habitual" = imperfective aspect stem, can be found in these
nominalized verb stems. In Ron-Daffo, -Bokkos, and -Sha, "progressives" and "future/in-
tentionals" are formed from these verbal nouns, whereas the "habitual" is formed from a
distinct and characteristically marked "aspect II" stem. In Ron-Kulere, the verbal noun
stem plays no role at all in the AUX system: here the "progressive" is built on the same
"marked" verb base as the "habitual". In Ron-Fyer, however, the apriori postulate of
aspectual dichotomy leads to the following untenable analysis:

> "Das Fyer unterscheidet zwei verbale Grundstammformen, die hier Aspekt-
> stamm I bzw. II genannt werden. Aspektstamm II dient gleichzeitig als
> hauptsächliches Verbalnomen in der Sprache. Aspektstamm I hingegen ist
> rein verbaler Natur und bringt grundsätzlich die punktuelle Handlung zum
> Ausdruck. Im übrigen erscheint der ursprüngliche Charakter der beiden
> Aspektstämme—ursprünglich im Sinne einer gemeinsamen Ron-Sprachgeschichte
> —stark verändert. So wird im Fyer der Aspekstamm II nicht nur zur Bildung
> der imperfektiven Formgruppen Habitativ und Progressiv, sondern auch für
> das Perfekt herangezogen. Die Kräfte für diese 'Verwirrung' dürften aus
> dem das Fyer umgebenden Angas stammen." (pp. 61-62).

Looking at the data from a non-biased point of view it seems to be more likely that Fyer has
lost the proto-Ron aspect II stem altogether and has established a FORMAL dichotomy without
semantic implications on the syntactic distinction of verb stem and verbo-nominal VN stem.
This cannot be compared with the situation in Kulere, where a SEMANTIC dichotomy seems
to be formally grammaticalized in the opposition of aspect I stem and aspect II stem. In
the three remaining languages of the group as described by Jungraithmayr, we do not find
a dichotomy but a trichotomy: aspect I stem/aspect II stem/VN stem. All three are
employed in the AUX systems of these languages. Cf. the chart which can be extrapolated
from the 1970 description, again using Jungraithmayr's original labels:

---

[4]Schuh (1976:11) has suggested that in those modern languages which have "two sets of
verbal nouns", historically, one of these is a reflex of a proto-Imperfective stem, while
the other is a reflex of the "true" proto-Verbal Noun. I disagree with Schuh only on
the respective verbal and verbo-nominal status of these stems: what he describes as
the "more verb-like" verbal noun (which he relates to the PC IPF stem) is, in my opinion,
a reflex of the PC VN (this is what Hausaists prefer to call the "primary verbal noun");
the more "noun-like" stems are, in my opinion, real nouns which originally do not belong
to the AUX system of the proto-language but which, at least in some modern Chadic
languages, are interchangeable with the VN in certain environments.

	ASPEKT I STAMM	ASPEKT II STAMM	VERBALNOMEN
BO	Grundaspekt(Aorist), Perfekt, Jussiv-Subj.	Habitativ	Progressiv, Futur
DA	Grundaspekt(Aorist), Futur I+II, Perfekt, Subjunktiv-Konsekutiv	Habitativ	Progressiv, Intentional
SH	Grundaspekt(Aorist), Subjunktiv, Futur, Perfekt I+II	Habitativ	Progressiv I+II, Intentional I+II
KU	Grundaspekt-Subj., Perfekt I+II, Futur-Ingressiv, Futur-Progressiv	Habitativ, Progressiv	
FY	ipf.Grundaspekt(Aorist I),Subjunktiv		prf.Grundaspekt (Aorist II),PerfektI+II, Habitativ,Progressiv, Temporalis

he theory of the fundamental binary distinction of aspect in Chadic as has been developed
o far subsumes a wide range of marking devices under the grammaticalization of the IPF:
egmental, suprasegmental, and syntactical. That these devices are genetically related to
ach other has to be taken for granted: the category which they are supposed to mark is
prioristically assumed to go back to even pre-PC times, i.e. the common ancestor of
roto-Chadic and Proto-Semitic (hence Jungraithmayr's frequent collocation of Chadic and
kkadian forms). As for the question of HOW these marking devices are related, he proposes
 four (possibly five) "stage model for the development of the Chadic languages" (in
ress b; cf. section 3 below). Occasionally (1970:62, in press a, 1976) he resorts to
he hypothesis of substratum influence to explain the change from segmental to supra-
egmental marking. Why in this theory segmental marking necessarily has to precede
uprasegmental marking can only be understood in the light of what was indicated above:
he aspectual distinction is viewed as a retention from Proto-Afroasiatic, and this lan-
uage was most certainly not a tone language, since tonal distinctions are held to occur
n only two families of the phylum, namely Chadic and Cushitic. Tone is thus most
omfortably attributed to the influence of genuine African substrata.

s it stands, the theory of the fundamental binary distinction of aspect in Chadic in terms
f unmarked perfective vs. marked imperfective, whether historically right or wrong, is
oo vaguely formulated to prevent it from being used as a catch-all concept without any
elevance for genetic subclassification and unsuited to draw inferences for the linguistic
istory of the Chadic languages.

2. THE MARKING OF MOOD, AKTIONSART, AND ASPECT (AUX) IN CHADIC

.1 THE PROTO-SYSTEM OF AUX-CATEGORY MARKING IN WEST CHADIC

ewman and Schuh (1974:7ff) have the following to say about West Chadic (= Plateau-Sahel
ere) AUX-category marking:

"So far we have been able to reconstruct four aspect marking morphemes for Plateau-Sahel. Since the presence of an overt marker in some aspects contrasts with ABSENCE of any overt marker in other aspects, we can treat phonological φ as itself being a marker. With this in mind, we can reconstruct the following: (1) *kà (or *kə̀), which indicated the Perfective; (2) and (3) φ, which was used both for a semantically less specific aspect labelled by German scholars "Grundaspekt" and for the Subjunctive; and (4) *àa, which indicated the Imperfective (Continuous, Future, and/or Habitual depending on the language) ....

"In addition to true aspect morphemes, many Chadic languages also make use of quasi-aspect marking morphemes derived from names of body parts in conjunction with one aspect marker or another....

"The third type of marking associated with aspectual differences in Chadic is a change in the verb itself. Two such verb stem changes can be tentatively reconstructed: a change in the final vowel of the verb to *i (or *e) in the Subjunctive; and the formation of 'habituative stems' (= Habitativstamm") by expansion of the basic form of the verb through suffixation or infixation of *awa (cf. Jungraithmayr 1966)."[5]

(Note: The term "aspect" as it is used here covers the whole range of AUX categories, in accordance with long established Anglo-American usage; cf. section 1.2.)

In a more recent publication, Schuh (1976) takes a modified standpoint compared to the 1974 study which was cautiously limited to P-WC, and postulates the validity of his insights for the whole of Chadic, including Biu-Mandara languages:

"In Newman and Schuh (1974) we reconstruct the following schema for the proto-Chadic verb complex:

PVP (+Prt) + Verb Stem   (PVP = preverbal pronoun

                                    Prt = aspect marking particle)

... I now question the inclusion of +Prt in the Chadic schema. There is little evidence for the reconstruction at any great depth of any such particle in the 'basic' verbal aspects [i.e. Subjunctive, Perfective, Imperfective—E.W.]. Newman and I reconstructed a *kV Perfective

---

[5]At the time of Newman and Schuh's writing, the accepted classification of Chadic languages was that presented in Newman and Ma (1966) which assumed only two branches for Chadic: Biu-Mandara (BM) and Plateau-Sahel (PS). In recent works, Newman (in press and 1977b) broke up PS into its two branches West Chadic (WC) and East Chadic (EC) which are understood to be "equally distinct from each other and BM, thereby setting up three coördinate branches for Chadic." For the purpose of this paper, I shall use all four terms—Biu-Mandara, Plateau-Sahel, West Chadic, and East Chadic—in the following way: now and then West + East Chadic will be jointly referred to as Plateau-Sahel, i.e. in the sense of Plateau-Sahel = Non-Biu-Mandara. I have adopted this usage to indicate that I consider it quite likely that on the basis of comparative grammatical evidence, compared to phonological and lexical evidence on which Newman's classifications are based, West and East Chadic do indeed constitute a valid linguistic entity within Chadic. If this should eventually turn out to be so ("Plateau-Sahel-Hypothesis") there is hardly another term better suited to label this linguistic entity because of the wide acceptance which 'Plateau-Sahel" has gained since it was first launched in Newman and Ma (1966).

morpheme and an *aa Imperfective morpheme.... As for the *aa Imperfective morpheme, ...I believe that this particle was, in origin, not part of the verbal system per se." (p. 7f)

This *aa, as Schuh continues to elaborate, was a general locative marker which was used in periphrastic constructions of the type 'be at doing'. Starting off from his insights into West Chadic languages, Schuh then hypothesizes on the Chadic situation as a whole:

"Unlike Hausa, many Chadic languages closely related to it mark aspect distinctions through modifications of the verb stem (whether internal changes or suffixes), not by particles between subject pronoun and verb. As already noted above, the verb in Hausa is invariable for most aspects. This is clearly an innovation in Hausa. Whether the use of aspect marking particles was necessitated by a shift toward invariance in the verb or verb invariance was allowed because of increased use of particles we cannot now say. In any case, the general Chadic picture conforms well to that for the rest of Afroasiatic, viz. a prefixed subject followed directly by a verb stem which undergoes modifications to show aspect distinctions." (p. 8)

(In the next section of this paper I shall demonstrate that indeed evidence from BM languages does conflict with Schuh's West Chadic evidence,[6] but that his reconstructions, nevertheless, come very close to what I believe can be assumed for the different proto-stages in the linguistic history of Chadic.)

When we try to represent Newman and Schuh's reconstructions for P-WC graphically, we end up with a model like the following,[7] using their own labels:

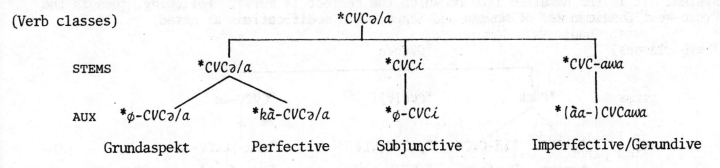

Fig. 5

Newman and Schuh do not appear to be too disturbed by the vagueness of their reconstructed Imperfective/Gerundive stem (which is expanded "through suffixation or infixation of *awa") as regards its syntactic status: is it a verb stem like the Subjunctive stem, or is it some kind of participle/gerund/verbal noun which is used in specific syntactical environment only? In a footnote the authors declare this to be an open question without attributing much significance to it:

---

[6] Schuh (1976:2): "As far as I know, the Biu-Mandara and East Chadic languages would not give evidence in conflict with that presented here."

[7] For simplification and illustrative purposes only the symbol *CVCV is introduced to represent ANY Proto-Chadic verb base. The "derived" forms of this basic symbol represent nothing but the TYPE of alternations which we can assume for the proto-stages.

"The infixal and suffixal stem formatives may well have been functionally
distinct, the one creating the true Habituative stem, the other forming
gerundives ..." (p. 8)

This statement obviously reflects the attempt to incorporate the concept of an expanded
stem which is said to be most typically marked by internal -$a(a)$-; explicit reference is
made in the text to Jungraithmayr (1966).

At the time, Newman and Schuh followed Jungraithmayr's line of argument in one further
point by interpreting some protoforms as paradigmatically related stem alternants, yet
only in the case of the Subjunctive stem (which Jungraithmayr neglects in his theory):
Newman and Schuh speak of "change in the verb itself", "formation...by vowel fronting",
"alternation". In the case of the proto-Imperfective stem (the formation of which Jungraithmayr likes to be treated as "apophonic"), however, Newman and Schuh speak of "infixation"
or "suffixation".

As regards the status of final *i of the Subjunctive stem, we shall not attempt to answer
the question whether a suffix -i was added to the lexical stem or whether *$CVC\partial/a$ and
*$CVCi$ represent paradigmatically related stem alternants. Our undecided position is re-
flected in putting the final vowel of the lexical stem in () when we give the Subjunctive
stem formula: $CVC(V)i$. Before we use the model based on Newman and Schuh for further
reference, we shall introduce the following terminological adaptions: instead of
"Grundaspekt" we shall speak of the Aorist aktionsart, instead of "Perfective" we shall
speak of the Perfect aktionsart, instead of "Imperfective/Gerundive" we shall speak of
Imperfective set of aktionsarten or verbal noun stem.[8] The verb stem which does not contain
any added elements and displays the final vowel contrast of the lexical verb classes we
shall call the "lexical" stem. This lexical stem functions as the Aorist in the AUX-
system. It is the unmarked item on which the Perfect is built. Following, then is the
Proto-West Chadic model of Newman and Schuh, with modifications as noted:

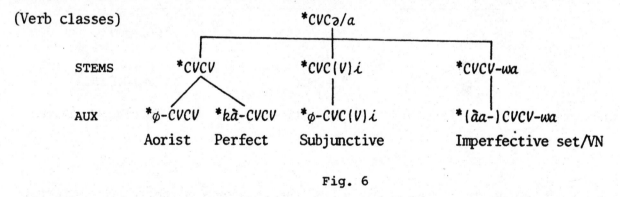

Fig. 6

This P-WC model, according to Newman and Schuh, may already represent a development from an
earlier (PC) system in which Imperfective and VN stems were distinct and had not yet merged.
The difference of the two stems lay in both morphological and syntactical features: the
Proto-Imperfective stem was marked by infixation and was a genuine verb stem, whereas the
Proto-VN stem was marked by suffixation of a phonologically similar morpheme and was used,
because of its verbo-nominal nature, in both verbal and nominal constructions. Accordingly,
the earlier PC model can be graphically represented as follows:

---

[8] The term verbal nouns as it is used in this paper denotes a syntactic "hybrid" insofar
as it is applied to stems which are to be classified as verbo-nominals, i.e. having the
features [+vb, +nom]. These stems are to be compared to "true verb stems" [+vb, -nom] and "true"
noun stems [-vb, +nom].

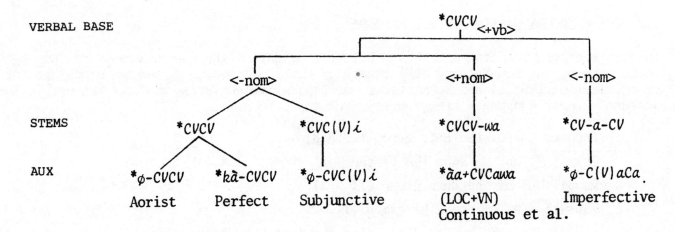

Fig. 7

Schuh (1976) finds himself in agreement with one of Jungraithmayr's positions insofar as he reconstructs the PC "Imperfective" stem as *CaCa* contrasting with the lexical stem *CVCə/a* and the Subjunctive Stem *CVCi*. In order to account for many, if not most, verbal systems in modern Chadic languages, Schuh has to assume some kind of syntactic change + merger:

> "Throughout much of Chadic, the Imperfective aspect and this locative construction [i.e. noun/pronoun + *aa* + nominalized verbal construction —E.W.] have fallen together. As the merger of these two constructions took place, certain formal characteristics of the locative construction won out. In particular, the Imperfective stem was reinterpreted as a type of verbal noun ..." (p. 10f)

Newman (1977a) seems to be inclined to take the "Proto-West-Chadic" model on p. 16 to be quite a likely picture of the situation already found in PC insofar as there were only three verb stems among which the stem ending in *-wa* was the proto-language's "Imperfective stem" (which later took over verbo-nominal features). In the view expressed by Newman (1977a), the so-called "internal changes" (for instance vowel change to *a*) can be explained by regressive assimilation from this very suffix *-wa* which, in some languages at least, later was dropped and thus created apophony-like phenomena in some modern Chadic languages.

Despite the wealth of Jungraithmayr's publications on this subject, no clear picture can be inferred as to what he actually believes the PC verb system to have looked like as a system: (a) he does not give any consideration to the separate status of the subjunctive (very early, in 1966, he assumed the subjunctive to belong to the same set of tenses as the Grundaspekt; cf. also the Ron Grammar (1970)), and (b) he does not seem to be afraid, just as Newman and Schuh (1974), to treat verbal nouns in modern languages and imperfective aspect stems as being basically the same thing without giving any consideration to the questions why and how they might be related.

My own position with regard to the proto-language's AUX-system will be elaborated further below. It is basically that of Fig. 6 with the interpretation that the stem ending in *-wa* was the proto-language's verbal noun. This means that I do not accept the existence of an imperfective verb stem BESIDE the VN stem. According to my own theory, the "noun-like" verbal nouns referred to by Schuh (1976:11f) in languages with "two sets of verbal nouns" ought to be treated as "deverbative nouns", i.e. as having the features (-vb,+nom), whereas the "verb-like" verbal nouns are reflexes of the proto-VN, i.e. having the features (+vb,+nom). Yet, for some Chadic languages I assume an innovative imperfective verb stem development through redesignation of the verbal noun or of plural verb stems (cf. 2.3.1).

2.2 AUX-CATEGORY MARKING IN BIU-MANDARA

In this section, ten languages which belong to eight of the eleven groups of languages which make up the Biu-Mandara (BM) branch of Chadic according to Newman's most recent classification (1977b) are submitted to a comparative analysis of their respective AUX-systems. These languages are, roughly from south to north:

Bachama (BA of the Bata group (II.A.8)

Tera (TE) and Ga'anda (GA of the Tera group (II.A.1))

Margi (MA) of the Bura group (II.A.2)

Kapsiki (KA) of the Higi group (II.A.3)

Lamang (LA) and Wandala (WA—also known as "Mandara") of the Mandara group (II.A.4)

Gisiga (GI) of the Matakam group (II.A.5)

Musgu (MU) of the Musgu group (II.B.2)

Logone (LO) of the Kotoko group (II.B.1).

A common stock of AUX-categories can be established for all of these languages. The corresponding verb forms are predominantly marked by preverbal particles. Yet, odd observations concerning the tonal behaviour of either verb stem or preverbal subject pronoun, or both, create the impression that preverbal marking by segmental morphemes is a more recent development which appears to be built on top of a more ancient system of suprasegmental marking: tonal distinctions with a segmental marking system superimposed show up in Lamang, Wandala, Logone, and perhaps Margi—less clearly in Gisiga and Musgu.[9] This section is, therefore, subdivided as follows:

Subsection 2.2.1 contains the outline of the verb systems as they are described by the various authors for the ten selected BM languages. Subsection 2.2.2 is devoted to a closer look at the question of suprasegmental AUX marking devices in BM. In subsection 2.2.3 we shall deal more extensively with the segmental marking devices in the AUX-systems and attempt to reconstruct the P-BM AUX-system. Subsection 2.2.4 is devoted to concluding remarks on the question whether P-BM had a dichotomous aspect system in terms of perfectivity or not.

2.2.1 AUX-Category Marking Systems in Modern BM Languages

2.2.1.1 Bachama

According to Carnochan (1970), Bachama has at least five aktionsarten in the affirmative. These are, in his terminology:

1. Perfect   4. Continuous
2. Past   5. Habitual
3. Future

plus a Repetitive (6.) and a Past Anterior (7.) of which only a few examples are available.

(1.) and (2.) share a common Negative Tense, so do (4.) and (5.). The Perfect has no segmental marker or, as we could say, contrasts with the other aktionsarten through absence of a segmental marker (ϕ-); the verb tone is always [-Hi].

---

[9]These are at the same time the northerly languages of the sample. Whether this geographical distribution has true historical implications or is rather accidental shall not be explored further here. For another instance of areal groups within BM compare the geographical distribution of REP/HAB stems (cf. 2.2.3.4).

The Past has a preverbal marker $\acute{a}$, the verb tones are either [+Hi] or [+Lo], never Mid
(= $\begin{bmatrix} \text{-Hi} \\ \text{-Lo} \end{bmatrix}$).

The Future has a preverbal marker *ɓáa*, the verb tones are those of (2.).

The Continuous has a preverbal marker *née*, the verb stem ends in *-i* (dropped before a following object), the verb tones are those of (2.).

The Habitual has a preverbal marker *dú*; there is no information on the quality of the stem final vowel if the verb is not followed by an object, the verb tones observed in the limited data[10] are different from both (1.) and (2.): Mid and [+Hi]!

The Repetitive has a preverbal marker *táa*; one of the four stems[11] contained in the data does not end in *-i*, three do; the verb tones are those of (2.).

There is only one example of the Past Anterior which is marked by preverbal *ɓée*; the verb does not end in *-i*, and the tones are those of (2.).

The Imperative is marked by higher pitch and greater pitch intervals (Carnochan's "Extended Register"). The verb stem, if not extended by suffixes or followed by an object, appears to end in *-i*, with tones as in (2.). There is no mention of a "subjunctive" paradigm. With regard to the verb stems themselves, we may provisionally summarize that they can be cross-classified according to final vowel substitution and tone patterns:

	-Hi	+Hi/+Lo	-Lo
-V	Perfect	Past Future (Repetitive) Past Anterior	? Habitual
-i		Imperative Continuous Repetitive	

2.2.1.2 Tera

According to Newman (1970), within the AUX-system of Tera we have to set apart the Continuous from all the other categories. This tense is marked by nominalizing the verb stem and inserting a preverbal marker $\acute{a}$. The Continuous may not be marked further for additional AUX-features.

Among the remaining AUX-categories the Subjunctive, Perfective, Future, and Sequential are marked by preverbal particles and may be further marked by additional preverbal morphemes for Habitual or Delayed Action. Markers of these two latter categories may not occur without any of the aktionsart markers. There is a preverbally unmarked stem used in the Relative Perfect. The Imperative is marked by stem final vowel alternations *ə > u* and *a > o*.

---

[10]Only three examples are quoted in Carnochan (1970:100) all containing the same verb.

[11]The preverbal marker *táa* is illustrated by three examples of the Repetitive Tense and one Past Anterior Tense. The distribution of stem-final *-i* does not correspond to this observation.

The preverbal markers are

á for the Continuous,   *kâ* for the Future,

kɔ̂ for the Subjunctive,   *tɔ̂* for the Sequential,

wâ for the Perfective,

plus   *kâ* for the Habitual,

                ɓâ for Delayed Action.

The category of Delayed Action has not been found elsewhere in BM.

2.2.1.3 Ga'anda

According to R. Newman (1971), Ga'anda, just like the closely related Tera, has two sets
of aktionsarten and shares furthermore the feature that these may be additionally marked
for Habitual "aspect" (with the same exception: the Continuous).

The first class of aktionsarten to be set apart for syntactical reasons contains the Continuous and Future, both built on the nominalized stem of the verb. Continuous is marked
by absence of a preverbal morpheme, Future has *na* followed by subject pronoun in front of
the verb stem (this *na* is etymologically related to the verb 'be' in Ga'anda). The
Future may be additionally marked for Habitual, the Continuous may not.

The second set of aktionsarten contains the

Aorist   marked preverbally by ϕ

Perfective   marked preverbally by   *ə*

Subjunctive   marked preverbally by   *kə.*

The Imperative   is marked by stem-final *-u.*

All of these can be additionally marked for Habitual by inserting preverbally the morpheme
tlə.

When using the verbal noun form in the Continuous and the Future, subject pronouns occur
before the verb, otherwise a set of suffixed pronouns is used (in the case of the Future,
it is this set of suffixed pronouns which is attached to the auxiliary verb 'be' and thus
occurs in pre-main-verb position).

2.2.1.4 Kapsiki

According to Smith (1969), among the various preverbal morphemes which mark AUX-categories
in Kapsiki, those which cannot immediately be recognized as "auxiliary verbs" used in
quasi-serial verb constructions, are the following in Smith's terminology:

ʔa·   Active Marker, if used with an otherwise unmarked verb stem it indicates "optative";

kɛ̂   Perfective Indicator, without any other markers it forms gerunds and/or perfective
        participles and is used in the negative perfective;

ka   Imperfective Indicator, used without any other markers it indicates non-completed
        action, habitual action, or purposive relation to a foregoing action;

te   Potential Indicator, "marks the time of an action relative to the agent's present"
        (cf. Tera Sequential);

ya   Continuous Aspect Indicator; "possibly this morpheme is the same one used as a
         copula before certain prepositions ... and as a relator between some emphatic
         pronouns and a verb" (p. 124fn.);

pa   Consecutive Sequential Indicator;

me   Indicator of a State Interrupted by an Action, (cf. the Gisiga participial prefix
         mV- in Lukas (1970) and Jaouen (1979));

kwa   Completive Sequential Indicator;

nda   Incomplete Sequential Indicator.

Verbs may be also used without any preverbal marker in Kapsiki, in the Imperative and when
used as "statives".

The various combinations of preverbal markers can be shown by the following chart with the
necessary addition that *te* may combine with preceding *kê*, *ka*, and *nda*:

	φ	kê	ka
nda	+	+	+
ʾa	+	+	+
pa	+	-	+

One further syntactic feature of the Continuous is worth mentioning: in this construction
the object precedes the verb whereas it normally follows the verb.

2.2.1.5 Margi

According to Hoffman (1963), Margi has the following aktionsarten which can be divided into
two groups with regard to the tonal behaviour of the so-called "changing verbs":

(a)   forms with a low-tone pattern:
      imperative, aorist, progressive, narrative

(b)   forms with a high-tone pattern:
      present, past, subjunctive

(For the purpose of this paper we disregard the negative forms "negative past" and "exclusive"
as well as the "infinitive" and its use as "conjunctive". Except for the "exclusive" which
is the negative subjunctive, all forms show the low-tone pattern on changing verbs.)

A significant accompanying feature of the forms with high-tone pattern, which Hoffmann does
not generalize upon, is the occurrence of immediate preverbal *a-*. Whereas all other
formations are marked preverbally (or by absence of a preverbal marker), the past is formed
from the present by adding a suffix to the verb stem. (This reminds us of Ga'anda where
the Sequential is formed by a suffix as opposed to preverbal morphemes in the other
categories.) The formation of the progressive can be set apart for syntactical reasons:
it involves a locative construction based on the use of the verb stem as a nominal, i.e.
verbal noun.

We can therefore classify the stems used in the Margi AUX-system according to phonological
and syntactical features, whereby the phonological feature of high-tone pattern is
accompanied by the morphological feature of a prefix *a-*. It must be borne in mind that
the tonal differences only appear in the case of the class of changing verbs. We may
therefore attribute the marking by *a-* prefix a greater functional load in modern Margi:

	verbal	verbo-nominal
ϕ (Lo tone)	imperative aorist narrative	progressive
a- (Hi tone)	subjunctive present (past)	

One further syntactical observation is worth mentioning which could be used as a criterion for further subclassification of forms: it concerns the position of the subject pronouns. We observe three types of conjugational forms with regard to this feature:

   (i)   post-verbal position of pronominals:

       imperative (if we include the plural indicator -*am̃*(*ə*) under "pronominals")

   (ii) pre-verbal position of pronominals:

       narrative
       subjunctive

   (iii) pre- or post-verbal position of pronominals:

       aorist
       progressive
       present, (past)

Pre-verbal position implies occurrence to the left of the respective aktionsart markers as well.

The preverbal AUX-markers are for the first set of stems

ϕ for the aorist,

gá   for the narrative,

ɔ̀vàr(< *wú+ìvì+r* "in-place-of") for the progressive;

for the second set of stems which are marked by preverbal *a*-

ϕ for the present (and past),

kɔ̀ for the subjunctive.

Since the subjunctive may be used without the preverbal particle *kɔ̀*, different sets of pre-verbal subject pronouns are used to distinguish subjunctive and present.

As regards the expression of perfectivity in Margi, Hoffmann (1963:116) summarizes the situation as follows:

    "The difference between the perfective and the imperfective aspects is
    closely connected with the difference between simple and derivative verb
    stems. For the transitive use of the verb, at least, it can be assumed
    that the simple verb stem is imperfective, while the derivative stems
    generally speaking are perfective. Intransitive verbs apparently can
    be used also perfectively in their simple stems, but sometimes derivatives
    are used, it seems, to stress the fact of completion."

2.2.1.6 Lamang

According to my own materials, the Lamang AUX-system is based on a primary distinction of stems with regard to their syntactic status: verb stems and verbo-nominal stems. Semantically, this distinction can be paralleled by the opposition of non-imperfective (verb stems) and imperfective (verbo-nominal stems). Within the non-imperfective aktions-arten set, three subjunctives can be set apart, two of which are marked preverbally and by high-tone pattern, the other by ϕ and low-tone pattern. The remaining forms in the non-imperfective can be divided according to whether they involve reduplication of the verb root or not. Reduplication of the verb root can be analyzed as marking perfective aspect: four aktionsarten are built on a reduplicative basis. The imperative, for morphological reasons, can be grouped with the ϕ marked subjunctive.

Within the set of non-imperfective aktionsarten which are all built on a verbal basis we find

I. unmarked morphologically and tonally

   aorist (= the lexical verb stem)

II. marked tonally and morphologically by

ϕ + Lo tone pattern	imperative, subjunctive$_1$
$\hat{a}$ + Hi tone pattern	subjunctive$_2$ ("perfective subj.")
ka + Hi tone pattern	subjunctive$_3$ ("repetitive subj.")

III. reduplicative formations additionally marked by

Hi tone pattern	perfect$_1$
Lo tone pattern	perfect$_2$ ("imperfective perfect")
$-ta-$ + Hi tone pattern	habilitative (= 'be able to')
$t\hat{a}$ + $-ta-$ + Hi tones	iterative habilitative

(The subjunctive$_3$ appears to be restricted to extended/derivative verb stems only and as such, possibly has to be fully specified as "perfective repetitive subjunctive".)

Within the set of imperfective aktionsarten which are built on a verbo-nominal basis we find

IV. Lo tone pattern stems additionally marked by

ϕ	imperfect (= the verbal noun)
ka	repetitive (cf. subjunctive$_3$!)
$\acute{\eta}$	progressive (cf. $\acute{\eta}$ 'in, into')
$t\hat{a}gh\bar{a}$	ingressive ($t\hat{a}gh\bar{a}$ 'on-top-of')
gu + pronoun	narrative-consecutive

V. Hi tone pattern stems additionally marked by

ϕ	durative
$t\hat{a}$	iterative (cf. iterative habilitative)

A number of these aktionsarten may additionally mark time reference by a preverbal morpheme da for future or sa for past. Subject pronouns are always suffixed to the stem, the only apparent exception being the formation of the narrative which synchronically has to be analyzed as containing an auxiliary verb *gu*.

Hoffmann's observations concerning perfective/imperfective in Margi (2.2.1.5) and Smith's on general/particular in Kapsiki (cf. fn. 16) seem to be valid for Lamang as well: the use of derivative extended verb stems/verbo-nominal stems is connected to the notion of completed action (aimed at or achieved), the use of simple non-derivative verb stems/verbo-nominal stems indicates non-completion insofar as it is the unmarked category in the system.

2.2.1.7 Wandala

According to Mirt (1971), Wandala has the following AUX-categories:

imperative	progressive	perfect
jussive	future	preterite

In Mirt's data the jussive is a subjunctive restricted to the 3rd person sg. and pl. The formation of negatives shall be disregarded here.

Reanalyzing Mirt's material, we can regroup the verb forms according to the following features:

(a) reduplicative vs. non-reduplicative formation

(b) position of subject pronoun (prefixed vs. suffixed to the first occurrence of the root in reduplicative formations)

(c) tone of prefixed subject pronoun

Reduplication plus incorporation of a suffixed subject pronoun (including the imperative plural indicator -*aw*-) is characteristic for the imperative/jussive/perfect. The jussive is additionally marked by a prefix $\hat{a}$-.

Reduplication of the verb root or its first radical consonant is in some cases connected to the derivative extension of the verb stem. This is the case in the progressive and a subset of preterite forms both of which use the prefixed subject pronoun for their conjugation. The main body of preterite forms, however, is found not to reduplicate the verb root even if it combines with derivative suffixes and/or suffixed object pronouns. We may thus provisionally distinguish preterite$_1$ from preterite$_2$ on the basis of this observation. The future in Mirt's corpus shows obligatory reduplication of the verb root which follows the prefixed subject pronoun. Strangely, no derivative stems have been found in this aktionsart by Mirt who indicates the possibility of a merger of future and progressive derivative forms (p. 57). As concerns the tones of the prefixed subject pronouns, we find Hi tones in future and progressive, and Lo tones in the preterites.

On the assumption of two mergers having occurred in the development of the Wandala AUX-system, we can represent the set of "prefix conjugations" in this language by the following chart, indicating formation and tone of subject prefix:

	simple stems		extended stems	
	-Redupl	+Redupl	-Redupl	+Redupl
preterite₁ preterite₂	} Lo		Lo Lo	
future progressive	Hi	Hi		} Hi

One further observation may be worth mentioning with regard to the verbal noun in Wandala. According to Mirt it is identical to the lexical verb stem and shows the same formational characteristics as do the stems in the preterite₂, and the progressive: it is non-reduplicative when using a simple, non-derivative stem, and it is reduplicative when using derivative extensions and/or suffixed object pronouns.

2.2.1.8 Gisiga

The two sources available for this language (Lukas 1970, Jaouen 1974) differ slightly with regard to the description of the AUX-system.

According to Lukas, the following categories are found:

   (i)   the imperative, generally unmarked but there are traces of a stem-final -u and
         a preverbal a-

   (ii) the aorist ("Grundaspekt") based on the lexical stem of the verb

   (iii) the future, marked by preverbal *sà*

   (iv) the progressive, marked by preverbal *rá*

Jaouen identifies these preverbal morphemes as etymologically related to the verbs *ru* 'go' and *so* 'come' and mentions for the Midjiwin dialect a *futur imminent* which uses two more "auxiliary" verbs (*wa < wi* 'commander, mesurer, estimer que, penser que'; *wud* 'vouloir'). Jaouen also mentions an aktionsart not observed by Lukas: a periphrastic habitual construction in which none of the above mentioned auxiliary markers may occur.

Both Lukas and Jaouen describe the perfect/*accompli* as being indicated by a postverbal morpheme *lè*. In Lukas' Gisiga this marker of completed action may co-occur with the aorist and the future (*futurum exactum*), but not with the progressive. In Jaouen's Gisiga, *lè* co-occurs with aorist (*inaccompli > accompli*), progressive, future, immediate future, but not with the habitual. Neither Lukas nor Jaouen have observed the use of the perfective postposition with imperatives. One further remark concerning the compatibility of this morpheme is worth to be quoted from Jaouen:

> "Le suffixe de l'accompli est incompatible avec la négation -*ta*. Dans
> le cas d'un accompli négatif, c'est le schème tonal seul qui renseigne
> sur son opposition avec l'inaccompli. L'accompli a un schème tonal
> haut, l'inaccompli a un schème tonal bas." (p. 16)

The tonal structure of Gisiga remains much of a mystery. Varying tones occur on both pre-verbal subject pronouns as well as on the stem itself. Cf. the following passages from Lukas (1970:62f):

> "In längeren Texten schwanken die Unterschiede der SP [i.e. subject
> pronoun - E.W.] im Ton beträchtlich. Auch hier ergibt sich kein
> völlig einheitliches Bild, und es muß damit gerechnet werden, daß
> gelegentlich die gehörten Töne falsch interpretiert wurden. Immerhin
> scheint aber die Tatsache erwähnenswert, daß eine Prüfung von 34
> Fällen, in denen die Aspektsituation klar ist, ergeben hat, daß der
> Tiefton der SP in 18 Fällen mit der Vorstellung der Dauer, des
> Zustandes und der Unvollendung verbunden war, während Hochton in 12
> Fällen auftritt, bei denen die Verbalform einen punktuellen Sinn
> hat.

> "Es ist ersichtlich, daß auch die Grundstämme Tonunterschiede aufweisen;
> ihre Wichtigkeit ist unbekannt."

In principle, the lexical stem of a verb may be used as a verbo-nominal. Rarely, Lukas
observed a verbal noun formation by prefixing a morpheme *a-*.

2.2.1.9 Musgu

According to Meyer-Bahlburg (1972), Musgu has an imperative/*Kohortativ*, an aorist, a future,
and a progressive. There are forms which look like the aorist but have optative/jussive
function in the dialect of Pus.

The aorist shows no overt marker. The tones on both the preverbal subject pronoun and the
verb stem itself vary, the function of these tonal changes is far from clear. However,
Meyer-Bahlburg observed a correlation of Hi tone and the notion of futurity/imperfectivity.

The future is formed by pre-posing an auxiliary *aga* which is etymologically related to *ga*
'go' to the complex of pronoun+stem.

The progressive is formed by pre-posing a finite form of the auxiliary verb *na* 'be' to the
stem of the main verb. Between the two a particle is usually inserted. There is con-
siderable variation as to which particle is used.

From the point of view of the syntactical environment, the stem of the main verb used in
the progressive constructions has to be interpreted as being the nominalized form, i.e.
the verbal noun. Meyer-Bahlburg admits this where she discusses prepositional particles
(p. 144ff), but ignores this fact when discussing the "verbal noun" (p. 129f). The formation
described under the heading of "verbal noun" is identical in shape to the plural stem of
the verb, i.e. marked by final *-i*. I consider it to be quite likely that this formation is
not that of a VN but rather that of deverbative nouns; cf. the following two forms from
the dialect of Pus, the first of which represents the general type of progressive in this
dialect, i.e. without any particle inserted between *na* and the main verb in the singular:

> *te na hala si*   'she is coming hither'
> she be go   hither

> *(won halai n) a na war hili-ni*   '(while) he was on his way'
> (while)   he be in go-his

Given the likelihood that the VN stem in Musgu has the same shape as the lexical verb stem
(as it is used in the aorist), there is no way to tell whether the periphrastic construction
of the future contains the lexical verb stem or the VN stem. One observation made by
Meyer-Bahlburg may deserve special attention. On p. 127 she notes that the verb *na* (but
only this verb) may add a morpheme *ka* which gives to the expression a preterite meaning:

múnì kə̀táy tɔ̀ náa ká tɔ̀ n áy vùrkɔ̀ tɔ̀dɔ̀bɔ̀ dâ

'it was the woman alone (*kətay*) she plucked out the mud (*todobo*)'

afut par mu na ka melɓeŋ

'previously (*afut par*) I was blind'

(The first example shows that *ka* has to be viewed as a postposition to *na* rather than a preposition to the following main verb.)

Completed action ("perfect") is indicated in Musgu by the use of one of two particles to the right of the verb: *lay/li* or *yaŋa/ya*. These postpositions co-occur with verbs in the aorist and the future (*futurum exactum*).

2.2.1.10 Logone

According to Lukas (1937), Logone has, beside the imperative, an aorist, a preterite, a perfect, a future, a continuous, and traces of a subjunctive.

The aorist has no overt marker, subject pronouns precede the verb stem. In the preterite, a marker *á* (*âa*) is inserted between subject pronoun and verb stem. A low tone on the complex of preverbal pronoun and marker may be used to indicate a "dependent" verb form, e.g. sequential, conditional, etc. The perfect is said to be marked by a verb suffix *-ya* (*-yaa*). In most cases, this verbal extension is used with preterite verb forms, i.e. having the preverbal marker *a* (*aa*). There are cases, however, where this extension occurs in the aorist or the future. The future and the continuous show a different structure: both make use of morphemes preposed to the subject pronouns and probably both of verbal origin: *sá-* (*sɔ́-*, *sa-*) for the future (cf. *sá* 'go out'), and finite forms of the verb *lì* ('be') for the continuous.

The subjunctive shows a preverbal morpheme *ka* before the complex pronoun+verb stem.

2.2.2 A Historical Hypothesis Concerning Suprasegmental Marking in the AUX-Systems of Biu-Mandara (BM) Languages

Too little is known about the tonal structure of BM languages to venture a satisfactory comparative study of verb tones in this branch of Chadic. However, even though we have to be very cautious in drawing conclusions from the scattered and incomplete information available, I consider it to be quite likely that the suprasegmental marking of AUX-categories on the verb complex, i.e. subject pronoun + verb stem, is a relatively ancient feature of the languages of the Biu-Mandara branch.

Only one possible interpretation of the data shall be tentatively presented here: the hypothesis that Hi tone pattern(s) on the verb complex could be used at an early stage in BM linguistic history to mark off (innovative?) derived categories, preferably in semantic areas which we now classify as being related to the notion of imperfectivity, e.g. "future" Time Reference, "continuous", "durative", "habitual" aktionsarten.[12] Our rather vague hypothesis rests on the following observations in 6 of the 10 selected BM languages.

---

[12]A less specific working hypothesis could be formulated, according to which Hi tone pattern marked off ANY AUX-category which was derived from already existing (Lo tone pattern) AUX-categories and vice versa, irrespective of the semantics of the categories involved, i.e. polar contrastive tone pattern as a general derivational marking device within the AUX-system of Proto-Biu-Mandara.

(1) In Bachama it is the Habitual which is set apart by an extraordinary tone pattern:
     Mid and Hi.

(2) In Margi, within the group of "changing verbs", it is the set of Lo tone aktionsarten
     which we are going to set up for Proto-Biu-Mandara, in contrast to which the Hi tone
     set (additionally marked by preverbal *a-*) can be considered secondary ("derived"):
     present, past, and subjunctive (secondary compared to the Lo tone imperative).

(3) In Lamang, within the imperfective set of aktionsarten, Hi tone pattern marks off
     the durative as well as the iterative aktionsarten.

(4) In Wandala, Hi tone on subject pronouns is associated with future and progressive.

(5) In Gisiga we are faced with apparently conflicting analyses: According to Jaouen,
     Hi tone pronouns followed by Lo tone verbs appear to be connected with *inaccompli*;
     Lo tone pronouns preceding Hi tone verbs seem to indicate *accompli*. According to
     Lukas, however, Lo tone on subject pronouns can be connected to duration, state, and
     incompleteness, whereas Hi tone on subject pronoun is associated with punctual meaning.

(6) In Musgu, Hi tone preverbal pronouns in the aorist are said to associate with the
     concepts of futurity or incompleteness. Whether this is also true for Hi tone pattern
     on the verb stem itself is less certain.

2.2.3 Historical Hypotheses Concerning Segmental Marking in the AUX-Systems of Biu-Mandara
       Languages and Reconstruction of the Proto-Biu-Mandara System

It has been mentioned before that the category of Time Reference (T) which is widespread
in BM and is also marked predominantly by preverbal morphemes, shall not be dealt with
in this paper from a comparative point of view. For our present needs it is sufficient to
state that all 10 languages which were analyzed do indicate T in one way or another. In
all 10 languages we find devices to mark futurity (whether as "future", "potential",
"ingressive", "intentional", or whatever the terms used in the grammatical descriptions
by the various authors), but only a minority appears to mark "past". Of the 10 languages,
7 have been found to indicate SQT, i.e. time reference relative to a preceding or following
action ("sequential", "consecutive", "past anterior", etc.) As regards those aktionsarten
which are common to the majority of BM systems, i.e. aorist, perfect, continuous, habitual/
repetitive, and subjunctive, we have to allow for a certain amount of semantic change and
overlapping with the category of time reference, especially in the cases of perfect and
"past", continuous and "future".

The aktionsarten as they are described by the various authors have to be re-labelled for
the comparative purpose of this paper, according to three principles:

1. All overtly or covertly marked VN stems are said to have an additional syntactic
    feature < +nom > and are set apart.

2. All overtly unmarked verb stems which cannot be assumed to contain the feature < +nom >
    are considered to be "lexical" verb stems and are classified as reflexes of the Proto-
    Biu-Mandara (P-BM) aorist.

3. Aktionsart function is attributed historical priority over Time Reference function for
    the time being, i.e. I shall assume for the purpose of this paper that P-BM AUX-
    markers may have developed into modern BM Time Reference markers but not vice versa.

Being able to formulate an hypothesis concerning the minimum inventory of aktionsarten
in P-BM does not mean that all the markers which we can reconstruct can be attributed the

same time depth. The linguistic history of aktionsart marking development did not stop
with the branching away of P-BM dialects from the rest of PC. P-BM cannot be assumed to
have encompassed a homogeneous dialect cluster, nor may this be true for the remaining
PC dialects. The first hypothesis, therefore, which I shall tentatively put forward is
that the marking of the Aorist, Perfect, and Continuous was basically the same in all
P-BM dialects, but that the devices to mark the Subjunctive and possibly another tense
category within the range of notions such as Repetitive/Habitual, were subject to further
developments in subgroups of P-BM dialects.

For the sake of easy reference and being aware of the gross simplifications involved, we
may graphically represent the P-BM situation—which is characterized by a tendency towards
invariability of the simple stem of any verb (which eventually affected the VN stem as
well)—as follows:

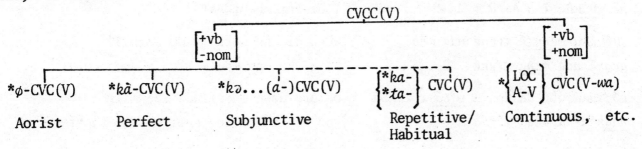

Fig. 8

(For explanation of symbols marked with * see 2.2.3.5 and 2.2.3.6.)

As indicated, this "reconstruction" of the P-BM mood and aktionsart marking system concerns
merely the shape of the verb stem and the preverbal markers. There is at least one further
device by which P-BM dialects may have indicated aktionsarten besides suprasegmental
marking, viz. position and choice of subject pronoun set. Within the frame of this paper,
this question shall not be further pursued. Only this much may be said here, that at some
stage in the linguistic history of P-BM dialects, position and shape of the subject pronoun may have served to distinguish at least the subjunctive from the indicative in the
category of mood.

In the following sections we shall now discuss the five "basic" aktionsarten of BM in
turn plus the formation of the verbal noun in this branch of Chadic.

2.2.3.1 The Aorist

The Aorist represents the UNMARKED unit in the system, both semantically as well as
morphologically. It corresponds to the "Grundaspekt" in Chadic literature. Being semantically unmarked means that the Aorist may encompass the functions of all other aktionsarten. Due to this general property of unmarked units it is quite likely that the Aorist
takes over the function of the Subjunctive where the latter is not overtly marked, as,
for instance, in Bachama, Gisiga, and Musgu (cf. Newman/Schuh (1974:7) for Grundaspekt
and Subjunctive in West Chadic). Morphologically unmarked stems being used in the
aktionsart system have been found in all languages of the sample.

In Bachama the unmarked verb stem is labelled "perfect" while the probable reflex of the
P-BM Perfect (see below) is labelled "past". The Aorist has acquired a rather restricted
usage in modern Margi's "aorist" which indicates "action of the past". (The functional
equivalent to the Aorist in modern Margi is the "present with prefix *a-".) In Wandala,
the AOR is hidden behind the Time Reference contrast of "future/present" and "preterite"
which is indicated by tone on the preverbal pronoun (Lo for <+past>, Hi for <-past>):

its unmarked nature is revealed when followed by a noun object and by the non-reduplicative morphology.[13]   In Gisiga and Musgu, the Aorist is subject to tonal variations.   In the following examples for reflexes of the P-BM Aorist the verb stems are underlined:

BA   hómon ǯ̆ì Fáɾe   'the chief has come to Fare'

        ndù ǯ̆ì   'he (it, m.) has come'

GA   kaɾ wandà sɜm-ta   'the boy refuses to eat'

        sɜn-mən naɸdì   'we know that man'

MA   ɫɜmà gɔ̆ ɾâ?   'where did you go?'

        nǐ shùwùnyǐ d Ástà   'I dreamt about Asta'

KA   xwéŋkwa menetê tɫenê nde wâà? 'when did he work (= do work)?'

        geŋkê nde mene tɫenê   'HE's the one who works (= does work)'

LA   kâdzúwâ vɜɫ dâdâmùkù pᵊsâ-ɫ t ûbâ 'before dawn one finds the milk'

        nâghâa-kâ bɜ̀gà tɔ̆kkâ ûɸ   'you see the place overgrown with trees'

WA   Nâmâdâ â-jà bɜɫsâ   'Namada kills a horse'

        but: â-jjà   'he hits, kills'

        tâ-jâmmê   'they gathered, joined each other'

        but: ŋâ-jâmmǐjê   'we (excl.) gathered, joined each other'

GI   kú ɫûm mê?   'what did you find?'

        ᵊà ŋgùm-àm dàw   'they cut Guinea-corn (each year)'

MU   tɜ̀ mɜ̀ɫâ   'she took'

        àdɔ̀ɫìyɔ̆ tɜ̆ yǐmâ ârùúŋ   'the hyena seized the boy'

LO   kâɫkadì a-wâ   'the book says'

        tâ i-wâ kǐ ...   'then they said that ...'

2.2.3.2   The Subjunctive

The Subjunctive represents a category which in modern BM languages appears as "optative", "jussive", "subjunctive", etc.   Except for Bachama, Gisiga, and Musgu, where the Aorist can be assumed to take over its functions (provided that there are no tonal distinctions!), the Subjunctive has been found overtly marked by a preverbal element in the languages of the sample; in Lamang (and Bura) we find both: segmentally marked and non-segmentally marked Subjunctive stems.

We find two possible reflexes of a P-BM Subjunctive marker: *kə and *a. *a seems to be restricted to immediate preverbal position as a true prefix to the verb stem, *kə appears to prefer a position to the left of the preverbal pronoun.

---

[13] In personal communication, Mirt gave examples of her own field materials on Wandala which show that the "future" of Lukas' material is rather a present or non-past, and that the lengthening of the initial radical in this tense is not present when the verb has a noun subject and object (there is also a change of tone on the verb stem).

Tera and Ga'anda both have *kə* which may co-occur with stems marked for habitual action.
In Margi, preverbal *kə* in position before the subject pronouns occurs exclusively with verb
stems marked by the prefix *a-* and may be omitted. The preverbal *ʾa* in position before the
subject pronouns of Kapsiki's "optative" synchronically appears to belong to an idio-
syncratic aspect <+active> in modern Kapsiki and is also used in "perfective" and "imperfective" verb forms. Lamang has a marker *ka-* (tone?) for a subjunctive of very restricted
use which seems to be in the process of merging with another prefix *ka-* (tone?) indicating
"repetitive action", nowadays denoting wish or command to repeatedly perform an action.
Whereas in Lamang, too, the Subjunctive may be expressed without any preverbal marking
(but tonally distinct from the unmarked Aorist), a "perfectivized" Subjunctive is marked
by preverbal *ã-* (plus again different tone pattern). Wandala's "jussive" shows a preverbal
marker *ã-*. (The imperative and the jussive of Wandala show the same kind of reduplicative
formation and subject pronoun suffixing as does the "perfect" in this language, an indication
of the perfective nature of the Wandala subjunctive?). Logone has a subjunctive prefix *ka-*,
again in front of the subjuct pronouns.

Especially in the light of the Margi, Kapsiki, and Lamang data I hesitate to relate all
"subjunctive markers" to a single P-BM morpheme. The CV forms may instead go back to
some kind of a prepositional particle which introduced subordinate clauses of some kind or
other; this would account for its pre-pronoun position in some, and its combinability with
other preverbal markers in other languages. (Such a particle *kə* is still used in Lamang.)

Whether the *a-* prefix was really P-BM or rather proto-Margi/Kapsiki/Lamang/Wandala/etc.
cannot be established. I believe that it was an innovation shared by only a limited group
of P-BM dialects.[14]

Provisionally, I have set up the P-BM Subjunctive as not being marked segmentally by a preverbal morpheme. This does not exclude the possibility of its being distinguished from
the Aorist by tonal differences and/or position and/or choice of pronoun set. Whether
languages like Bacama, Gisiga, and Musgu have retained the P-BM picture or have, secondarily,
lost any preverbal marker which they might have had at some stage, cannot be decided. Post-
P-BM developments shall be made responsible for the time being for the emergence of at
least two segmental subjunctive markers in modern BM languages:

(a)   Subjunctives with immediate preverbal *a-*:

MA   *sái g‿ã́-mãi kéŋkų̃!*   'you must go now!'
      ndã́ zə́m y‿ã́-wĩ!   '(wait) that I run, let me run!'
      ská y‿ã́-wĩ   'lest I run'

LA   *ã́-tsxũrãyõ*   'that I be seated'
         cf. *φ-tsxũrãyò*   'that I sit down'
      ká-skwébəd́ də́ vlãdã́!   'let him (repeatedly) come to my place'
         (< *kə-a-skwebedé* ?)

---

[14]There is still a lot of uncertainty about the origin(s) of the preverbal *a-* in BM
languages. We cannot dismiss the possibility of its being related to the PC Perfect
marker *kã̀* (2.2.3.3) in at least Lamang and Wandala: both languages mark completed action
by innovative reduplication and show no other traces of the PC marker *kã̀* unless in the
Subjunctive (which has strong perfective connotations, at least in Lamang). According
to my own field materials, the Perfect marker in the closest relatives of Lamang and
Wandala in the Mandara group (Guduf, Cena, Dghwedé, and Gvoko [in the negative]) has lost
its initial consonant and is thus identical in shape to the Subjunctive markers in Lamang
and Wandala.

WA   ằ-jằɾjằ (vb: ja)   'they should hit'
      ằ-ɗằbⱬiɗằbằ (vb: ɗaba)   'let him follow me!'

(b) Subjunctives with prepositional kə/ka:

TE   Aℓi kə nji dℓu   'Ali should eat meat'
      Aℓi kə ka nji dℓu   'Ali should eat meat (regularly)'

GA   kə kaɾ wanɗa səm-ta   'the boy should refuse to eat'
      kə tℓə ɾaka-ən ə waɫwuɾca   'you should (hab) run in the morning'

MA   sằi kə g‿ằ-mằi kềŋkʉ̰!   'you must go now!'
      k‿y‿ằ-wⱬ   'that I run, I should run'
         (cf. examples under (a) above)

KA   ʔa na gwenakḗ   [?]   'you must send [him]'
      ʔa ŋkḗ keℓte ɗằ ℓekwesá [?]   'he should take my shirt for me'

2.2.3.3 The Perfect

The Perfect is the aktionsart which indicates completed action in the past or an action aiming at ending with completion irrespective of time. Reflexes of its preverbal marker *kằ can be found all over BM. For semantic reasons, however, the Perfect may overlap with the Time Reference category "past" or have acquired "preterite" function in modern MB languages: in Logone, for instance, postradical -ya(a) which marks completeness of action in the system of thematic derivation, preferably occurs with verbs which are preverbally marked by ằ(a) and are labelled "preterite" by Lukas (1937:39f); in Bachama, however, stems with preverbal a- are labelled "past" by Carnochan who calls the unmarked stem "perfect" (cf. Aorist above). In the marking of "perfectivity" BM languages have gone different ways with regard to   lexicalization, but none of the 10 languages of the sample can be said not to mark <+prf> in one way or another.[15]

---

[15]One has to be careful not to confuse grammatical cateogries when it comes to analyzing expressions of "completed action". (1) We have to look out for potential grammaticalizations of Perfective aspect, only one of which may be the Perfect aktionsart; (2) We have to separate, for analytical reasons, such manifestations of AUX-categories from originally derivational categories such as "completive" verb stems which are marked by derivational suffixes; (3) We have to account for the possibility that verb stems which are thematically extended according to (2), are being used synchronically to mark aktionsart as in (1). To complicate the matter further, some BM languages (Margi, Kapsiki, Lamang, and according to personal information, possibly Wandala as well) share an aspectual dichotomy originally outside the scope of perfectivity but related to it semantically: this is the opposition of the two notions of GENERAL and PARTICICULAR (Smith 1969), by which simple, i.e. thematical non-extended verb stems are in contrast to extended, i.e. thematically derived stems. The GENERAL aspect shares certain semantic features with IMPERFECTIVITY, whereas PARTICULARIZATION shows strong affinity to PERFECTIVITY. A further intersecting category in these languages i TRANSITIVITY. To illustrate how these three dichotomies intersect we only have to re-phrase Hof mann's important passage from his Margi grammar (1963:116):

The difference between the PERFECTIVE and the IMPERFECTIVE aspects is closely connected with the difference between GENERAL and PARTICULAR. For the TRANSITIVE use of the verb, at least, it can be assumed that the GENERAL is IMPERFECTIVE,

The notion of perfect-ness in a number of BM languages is connected to "extension" of the
verb stem, either by thematic derivation via suffixes (Kapsiki, Margi, Gisiga, Musgu,
Logone), and/or by reduplicative morphology (Lamang, Wandala). Smith (1969) has related
this phenomenon to a semantic dichotomy of "general" vs. "particular", which means that the
very presence of a derivational suffix may already indicate perfectivity (cf. Hoffmann
(1963) for Margi), or at least imply the likelihood of perfective action (cf. Smith for
Kapsiki).[16] Yet, Margi seems to be the only language of the sample in which this relation
fully holds--it has no other means to indicate perfectivity than by thematic derivation (if
we exclude the use of "auxiliary verbs" such as 'finish' in quasi-serial verb constructions).
In BM in general, however, there seems to exist at least one derivational suffix, the only
function of which now appears to be the indication of completed action. Whether this was
the primary and historically original function need not concern us here. The specialized
suffixes or postpositions in the various languages may be etymologically related in some
instances. The increasing functional load of <+prf> marking by postradical devices may have
caused, eventually, the loss of the preverbally marked Perfect tense (for instance in
Lamang, Wandala, Gisiga, Musgu, and Logone) without the P-BM Perfect marker's being necessarily lost entirely. It may have become redesignated, restricted in use, or merged with
another preverbal marker. The identification of the P-BM Perfect marker *kà in Kapsiki
and Lamang/Wandala must be regarded as provisional. Kapsiki has a "perfective indicator"
kê in immediate preverbal position the functions of which also include the formation of some
kind of "participle".[17] If we assume that Kapsiki kê has resulted from a merger of P-BM *kà

---

while the PARTICULAR generally speaking is PERFECTIVE. INTRANSITIVE verbs
apparently can be used also PERFECTIVELY in the GENERAL, but sometimes PARTICULAR-
IZATION is used, it seems, to stress the fact of completion.

[16]The relevant passages in Smith (1969) are:

"The notion of general and particular is basic to an understanding of
event semology and the reflection of this in the grammar is what led
Hoffman [sic—E.W.] to contend that Kapsiki verb roots are basically
imperfective while stems are perfective. ["Root" in S.'s terminology
is the simple, non-derived stem, "stem" is the extended thematically
derived unit—E.W.] In fact, this is not strictly accurate even
though there is a statistical correlation between the use of extended
roots and perfective markers. The reason for this is simply that
stems are the realizations of particularized events and they can most
easily be so specified if they have already happened (completed
aspect) or are viewed as being under the control of the speaker (imperative mood)." (p. 110fn.)

"No general sememe of particular aspect appears to be realized and
thus if posited must be done so at a hypersememic level. (Possibly
the grammatical unit 'verb suffix' could be considered the realiza-
tion of such a sememe, but this seems not to be a fruitful approach,
since each suffix does realize a certain kind of particular.)" (p. 139)

". . . the sememe GENERAL is usually realized by the unextended use
of the verb." (p. 140)

[17]Kapsiki kê is used to (a) form the participle, indicating a state resulting from a
previous action, (b) express what would be translated into English as the "gerund" form
of the verb, (c) express the negative perfective, (d) express completed action in the
past (but here it is used in combination with an "active marker", among others: 'a), (e)
express doubt about the future completion of an action or to indicate that something should
follow its eventual completion. (Cf. Smith (1969:121ff)).

and a participial prefix, this might explain another anomalous behavior: its appearance in the negative. According to personal communication, Newman considers it a common feature of the Chadic Perfect marker that it does not co-occur with the negative marker. Kapsiki *kê*, however, does:

>   *kê-xeve kelepé xê wê*   'They didn't catch any fish.'

Lamang displays a contrast of <-prf>:<+prf> in the subjunctive, morphonologically apparent as ∅ + Lo tone verb stem vs. *â-* + Hi tone verb stem. We cannot dismiss the possibility that the marker *â-* here is a reflex of P-BM *kà* since there is no other reflex of this ancient marker to be found in the language. There is corroborating comparative evidence, too: P-BM *kà* seems to have lost its initial consonant in all languages of the "Mandara Group" as my own data on Guduf, Cena, Dghwede, and Gvoko suggest. Wandala, too, has no other reflex of P-BM *kà* other than possibly the "jussive" marker *à-*. The reduplicative morphology and the use of the suffixed pronoun set, both features of the Wandala "perfect", may serve as synchronic evidence for the analysis of the Wandala "jussive" as being a "perfective sub-junctive" comparable to the Lamang *â-* + Hi tone stem formation.

In Bachama and Logone, it seems, that the P-BM Perfect marker has lost its initial consonant, too, and is now being used to indicate "preterite" Time Reference. In Musgu, there is a morpheme *ka* which serves to indicate past time yet is restricted to co-occurrence with the verb *na* 'be' and used postverbally rather than preverbally (cf. 2.2.1.9).

Whereas in Ga'anda the initial consonant is also lost entirely, Tera, of the same group, has two allomorphs, one with and one without an initial consonant. Within the Margi-Bura group, voicing of the initial consonant seems to be restricted to Margi of Lasa. Bura, Cibak, Margi of Minthla, for instance, have a voiceless stop according to Hoffmann (1955) and Meek (1931).

Used as typological features, Perfect marking devices in the AUX-systems could serve for lower level subclassification within Biu-Mandara:

<+prf> in aktionsart systems			
INFLECTIONAL			DERIVATIONAL
pre-radical prepositional/prefix		radical redupl/tonal	post radical suffix/postposition
BA	+ (*â-*)		
TE	+ (*wà*)		
GA	+ (*ə*)		
KA	+ (*kê-*)		+
MA	+ (*gâ-*)		+
LA	? (*â-*)	+	+ (Hi)	+
WA	? (*à-*)	+		+
GI			? (Hi)	+ (*lê*)
MU			? (Lo)	+ (*li;ya*)
LO	+ (*â-*)			+ (*yâ*)

Following is a list of examples of possible reflexes of P-BM *kā in modern BM languages:

BA   hómon a ší Fare   'the chief came to Fare'
      ndá ší   'he (it, m.) came'

TE   Ali wà nji dlu   'Ali ate meat'
      Ali a à nji dlu   'Ali ate meat (there)'

GA   ə kar wanda səm-ta   'the boy refused to eat'
      ə tlə raka-kə-mən ə walwurca   '(then) we (hab) ran in the mornings'

KA   kê-mtê nyê nde   'she died (herself)'
      ʔa kê-satê   '(he) stood up'

MA   nǐ gà-wǐ   'I ran'
      dɔ̌ mǎlǎ gɔ̌ndǎ gà hɔ̀r tɔ̌lɔ̌m ...   'then his wife took the horn . . .'

LA   (cf. 2.2.3.2)

WA   (cf. 2.2.3.2)

LO   w-âa-mtǐ   'I died'
      w-âa-vi-yà   'I have stood'

2.2.3.4 The Repetitive and/or Habitual

The Repetitive and Habitual pose a problem in that there is no clear indication as to whether they originally constituted a single or two different categories. Grammaticalizations of the notion of repeated/iterative action are attested for the "southerly" languages of the sample (Bachama, Tera, Ga'anda, Kapsiki, and Lamang); no traces are found in Margi, Wandala, Musgu and Logone. In Gisiga the aktionsart Habitual has exceptional status in Jaouen's data; Lukas did not find it in the dialects which he studied.

As in the case of the P-BM Subjunctive, I hesitate to reconstruct one single morpheme as the P-BM marker. Rather, I assume that, although most if not all P-BM dialects may have had grammaticalizations of Repetitive and/or Habitual, different preverbal markers were being used for this category/these categories, or even none at all. If Repetitive and Habitual were in fact different categories at some stage in the linguistic history of Biu-Mandara, then *ta and *ka could have been the respective markers in at least some dialects of P-BM.

Kapsiki ka- is said to be more of a general "imperfective indicator" which, among other functions, serves to denote habitual action. (Habitual action can also be indicated by reduplicative "plural" verb bases in Kapsiki.) Lamang ka- (indicating repeated action in the past) is not frequently used, the predominant preverbal marker for iteration of action is ta-. The latter is probably cognate to Bachama tâa- "repetitive". Both Bachama and Lamang have two markers for repetitive and habitual (iterative) action—Bachama dú-/tâa-, Lamang ka-/ta-, respectively—and seem to use one each exclusively with "marked" verb stems (= VN, if the Bachama stem in -i turns out to be verbo-nominal). Tera and Ga'anda share the typological feature that in these closely related languages the Habitual marker may co-occur with both the Perfect and the Subjunctive marker.

BA	*nà dú gùr dawye*	'I keep horses' (Hab.)
	ndà jóŋò, táa ᵓùli	'he waded in and kept on searching for it' (Rep.)
TE	*Ali wà ka nji dlu*	'Ali eats meat (regularly)' (Perf. + Hab.)
	Ali kɔ ka nji dlu	'Ali should eat meat (regularly)' (Subj. + Hab.)
GA	*tlɔ raka-kɔ-mən*	'(when) we run' (Hab.)
	ɔ tlɔ raka-kɔ-mən	'(then) we ran' (Perf. + Hab.)
	kɔ tlɔ raka-ən	'you should run' (Subj. + Hab.)
KA	*ka-yidê dâ mbɔli*	'one makes fun of me'
	ka-memené tlenê nde	'he works all the time'
LA	*sà* {*kâ* / *kâ*} *-skwêb-xãŋ*	'they kept on coming'
	tɔ̀-mõn-kènì zɔ̀màn	'it is custom that you(pl) do the ritual farming'
GI	*yá ádà ì-rú*	'moi *il* y a je vais' = 'j'ai l'habitude d'aller'

2.2.3.5 The Continuous

The Continuous as a P-BM aktionsart is reflected in all 10 languages of the sample by periphrastic constructions, either using auxiliary verbs, locative particles, or both. We can
therefore assume that P-BM had already   lexicalized some sort of periphrastic construction
to express this aktionsart.

Some languages show what may be called segmental "markers" for the Continuous (Bachama, Tera,
Kapsiki, Margi, Lamang, Gisiga, Musgu, Logone) which all in fact may be nothing but originally
syntactic devices to build up this category, even where the morphemes cannot be immediately
related etymologically to auxiliary verbs and/or locative particles as in the majority of
cases.

In Wandala and Ga'anda we find no overt segmental marking device (indicated by ⌀ in the examples further below). Ga'anda, however, has fronting of subject pronouns in this aktionsart
making use of the disjunctive pronoun set. Fronting is also one of the features of the
Continuous in Kapsiki; in this language it affects direct objects. The Kapsiki marker *ya*
may, as Smith (1969:124) points out, be etymologically related to a certain copula used between some emphatic pronouns and the verb. Margi *ʔvɔ̀r* can, according to Hoffmann, be
analyzed as *wú* 'in' + *ìvì* 'place' in an *r*- genitive construction. As for Lamang, three
markers compete to indicate continuousness: (i) the prepositional complex *tagha* (< *ta+
ghaŋa*   'on+top-of') which denotes at times an ingressive notion ('be about to do'); (ii) the
prefix *ta-/tɔ-* which we have encountered already in connection with HAB/REP (2.2.3.4) as
a marker of iterative action with durational connotation (and which may be etymologically
related to the locative particle *ta* 'on, onto'); and (iii) the locative particle *ŋ̊* 'in'
which has rather low frequency of occurrence in the recorded materials. Gisiga *rã* can be
related to the verb 'go' (Jaouen). Musgu *n áy* (dialectal: *n aŋ*) is analyzed by Meyer-
Bahlburg as containing the auxiliary verb *na* 'be' + locative particle *áy/aŋ*. Logone uses an
auxiliary verb *li* 'be'. Bachama *nêe* may be ultimately related etymologically to a root
*n- 'be' in P-BM (cf. Ga'anda *na* as used as an auxiliary verb in the future, Musgu *na*, Lamang
na 'be invisibly present', Gisiga *ne*).

BA	*hɔ́mon nêe hiiwì*	'the chief is praying'
	sùnêe ŋŏl sàlakéy	'he is pulling the rope'

TE   Alí á njí dlu   'Ali is eating meat'
      Alí á gaɓ-tə   'Ali is returning'

GA   φ ŋgət kar səm-ta   'I am refusing to eat'
      φ wanda raka-ta   'the boy is running'

KA   gwambê ya-xe xê   'they were catching frogs'
      wupê ya-wupê yɛmú   'the water is boiling'

MA   nàg ə̂və̀-r wì   'you (sg) are running'
      yàmâd ə̂və̀-r psə̂   'the wind is blowing'

LA   a) skwêdî nà, tàghà-xə̂d màrkúmbàghà ⎫
      b) skwêdî nà, t-xə̂d màrkúmbàghà   ⎬
      c) ŋ̂-xə̂d màrkúmbàgh skwêdî   ⎭
                                                       'when I came down, your wife was grinding'

WA   yâ-φ-zâ   'I am eating'
      mî-φ-z-àtə̀r-za   'we are eating them'

GI   ʾí rá dè   'I am cooking'
      gòd ʾà rá wàs   'something is moving'

MU   kə̀ n ây mà sù-kù   'you wash yourself ("your body")'
      gùrnày à n ây bə̀dà slàakáy   'the lion is waiting for the cattle'

LO   m-a-li m-zəm   'we are eating'
      t-a-li i-zəm   'they are eating'

2.2.3.6 The Verbal Noun (VN)

The Verbal Noun is a syntactic category in all languages of the sample. Its shape is far
from uniform. Dubious are the cases of Bachama and Musgu. For Bachama we find only indirect
evidence that the segmentally marked verb stem in -i represents the VN of that language,
given the fact that the Continuous is built on this stem. Termination and usage in the
imperative, on the other hand, strongly suggest that this stem might be a reflex of the PC
modal stem which we have reconstructed as *CVC(V)i—a case of merger of the two marked stems
of the proto-language? For Musgu see 2.2.1.9: a-stem and i-stem both occur in the verbo-
nominal slot of the Continuous construction, the i-stem being the language's plural verb
stem and, as it seems to be, the citation form ("infinitive") of a verb. The question
which we cannot answer at present is therefore: is the infinitive actually the plural verb
stem or is it a deverbative noun formation in -i which accidentally looks so much like
the verbal plurals? I am inclined to think that i-stems have nothing to do with verbal
nouns in Musgu, and that the latter are not marked overtly in this language.

Segmentalized nominalizers are found in 5 of the 10 languages. In 4, however, the VN marker
has a zero allomorph. In three (four if we include Musgu) languages "zero", i.e. absence
of any segmental marking device makes it impossible to distinguish the verbal noun from the
lexical stem other than by syntactical environment: Margi, Gisiga, Logone, and possibly
Musgu are the languages without overt VN marking.

Lamang and Wandala use allomorphs of their respective VN markers according to whether the
verb stem to be nominalized is simple or thematically derived:

	simple stem	extended stem
Lamang:	-o (< *-wa?)	-ta
Wandala:	∅	REDUPLICATION

In Tera, Ga'anda, and Kapsiki a morpheme *ta* which is very likely cognate to the extended
stem suffix -*ta* in Lamang, contrasts with its absence under certain syntactic conditions.
Only for Ga'anda this morpheme is described explicitly as "nominalizer", in Tera it is
referred to as "linker", as is its function in Kapsiki. We therefore assume that the morphe
ta in P-BM was not a nominalizing suffix but a gender-sensitive (feminine gender) linking
particle following the verbal noun under certain specified conditions—possibly substituting
the original verbal noun suffix in these environments:

       *CVC(V)-wa + *ta* + X ---→ *CVC(V) *ta* X

In Lamang and Ga'anda the linker later developed into a suffix ("nominalizer", restricted to
extended stems in Lamang).

With the exception of Lamang, the original VN suffix was lost in the other nine BM languages
probably as a result of the general tendency in this branch of Chadic to give up stem-final
distinctions altogether. In order to reflect this development, we shall indicate the widespread loss of the suffix in our reconstruction diagrams by the symbol *CVCV(-wa).

For examples of VN in context see Continuous examples at the end of section 2.2.3.5.

2.2.4 Conclusion: Did Proto-Biu-Mandara Have a Dichotomous Aspect System in Terms of Perfectivity?

When we "reconstruct" the P-BM AUX-system we find no evidence for the proto-language's
having its aktionsarten neatly organized in two sets according to certain recurring
morphological features the primary function of which ought to be seen in marking an aspectua
dichotomy in terms of perfective/imperfective.

In modern BM languages we find at least three dichotomies in the AUX-systems:

    1. modal dichotomy: Indicative vs. Subjunctive;
    2. aspectual dichotomy: General vs. Particular;
    3. syntactic dichotomy: Verbal vs. Verbo-Nominal

All three dichotomies could be semantically related to the notion of perfectivity insofar as
Subjunctive mood and Particular aspect (= the use of extended verb systems) show affinities
with the Perfective, and the use of the VN within the aktionsart system is associated with
Imperfective connotations. As for the affinity of Subjunctive mood and Particular aspect
to perfectivity, Smith (1969) offers an explanation. According to his observations in
Kapsiki, extended verb stems are the realizations of "particularized events", and these can
be most easily be so specified if they have already happened (Smith: "completed aspect")
or are viewed as being under the control of the speaker (Smith: "imperative mood"). As
regards the proto-language of the Biu-Mandara branch of Chadic, I assume all three dichotom
i.e. that of Indicative/Subjunctive, General/Particular, and Verbal/Verbo-Nominal to have
been properties of P-BM, together with their respective connotations with regard to perfectivity. A simple dichotomy of Perfective/Imperfective as higher level classifications o

aktionsarten, however, cannot be reconstructed for Proto-Biu-Mandara.

2.3 THE PROTO-SYSTEM OF AUX-CATEGORY MARKING IN CHADIC

This section is devoted to the development of hypotheses concerning the minimal properties
of PC's AUX-category marking system, and to the proposal of a theory to account for the
ways in which this "reconstructed" system developed in the course of the linguistic
history of Chadic. I shall follow the same approach as before, i.e. the inductive extrapo-
lation of the common denominators of systems, i.e. of the proto-system-models which we
have discussed in the previous sections of this paper (Figs. 6-8).

According to the theory presented here, all PC dialects shared at least three distinct
verbal stems which were used in their AUX-category marking systems:

> 1. the "lexical" stem
>
> 2. the "modal" stem
>
> 3. the "verbo-nominal" stem

These three stems were structurally related along the lines of a number of dichotomous distinctions:

(a) In terms of markedness, the modal and the verbo-nominal stems were both marked as
     opposed to the lexical stem.

(b) In terms of syntactic subcategorization, the lexical and the modal stems were both
     truly verbal as opposed to the verbo-nominal nature of the VN stem.

(c) In semantic terms, the use of the lexical and the verbo-nominal stems in the mood
     system can be subsumed under "Indicative" usage in contrast to the usage of the modal
     stem in the "Subjunctive(-Imperative)" mood.

The three stems were the basis for the formation of the various aktionsarten which were
principally marked preverbally either by existence or absence of segmental morphemes. Of
the preverbal markers (there may have been several, but we do not yet know how many and
what their shapes were), only one can be reconstructed with confidence for the time being:
the Perfect marker *$k\tilde{a}$ which was used in combination with the lexical stem. Without any
preverbal marker, the lexical stem served to indicate the unmarked aktionsart which we have
called Aorist.

The simple, i.e. non-extended modal stem was marked by high vowel stem termination (reconstructed as *-i) and was very likely used without any further marking of aktionsart or
time reference in preverbal position.

The simple verbo-nominal stem was marked by a suffix *-wa. When used in the aktionsart
system of the proto-language, the VN had to be embedded in periphrastic constructions which
were formed with the aid of either "auxiliary verbs" ('be', 'go', etc.) or locative particles ('in', 'at', 'on top of', etc.) or both. These periphrastic constructions were used
to indicate actions in progress, actions about to happen, duration of state, and possibly
similar semantic notions.

In addition, although outside the actual AUX-category marking system, the proto-language had
a number of other devices to modify verbal meanings, such as thematic derivation by extension of the stem to the right (suffixation), the formations of verbal plurals by augmen-
tation of the phonological inventory of the verbal base itself. Choice and position relative
to the verb stem of subject pronouns may also have been a mechanism at the disposal of

speakers of PC dialects, and almost certainly a number of auxiliary verbs beside the ones used in periphrastic aktionsart formation could enter so-called serial verb constructions. Of these various devices to modify the meaning of a verb in the proto-language, the first two, i.e. stem extension and plural formation, were the most likely to be made use of in the further development of the aktionsart differentiation towards the marking of completed and/or non-completed action, i.e. towards the development of perfectivity as an aspectual category. The proto-language may have already possessed extension suffixes to indicate "completive" or "incompletive" action which set the semantic frame for such a development, and the usage of verbal plurals in modern Chadic languages suggests that PC may have already used these to indicate frequentative/repetitive/habitual/etc. action. If we follow Schuh on one of his imaginative journeys into Chadic language history, we could image the preverbal Perfect marker *kà to have originated from an originally post-verbal derivational suffix denoting "completive" action; cf. fn. 2 in Newman/Schuh (1974:7).

The following diagram may serve to represent the "reconstructed" PC mood and aktionsart marking system:

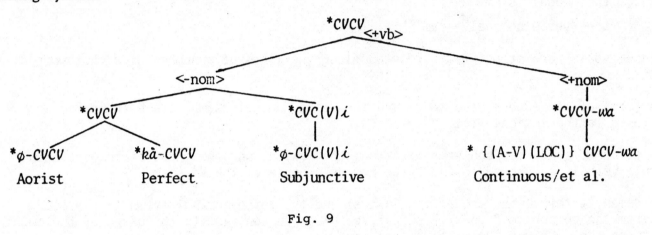

Fig. 9

If, however, we prefer to look at the system from a semantic rather than syntactic point of view we may represent the PC situation by Fig. 10 which is just a variation of Fig. 9:

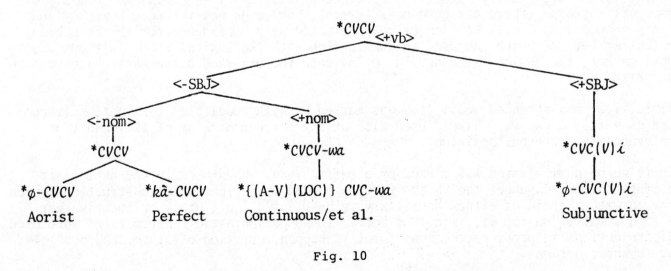

Fig. 10

2.3.1 The Emergence of the Imperfective in Plateau-Sahel

The PC aktionsart system was not at all insensitive to perfective and/or imperfective connotations of certain formations, as we had reason to point out previously. Most of all verbal plurals when they were used to indicate repeated/frequentative/habitual action, which are outside the actual aktionsart system per se, and the VN-based periphrastic constructions, which indicate continuous/durative/future action or state, can be assumed to have had quite strong imperfective connotations. Common to all PC dialects may have been a "drift" toward paralleling the marked Perfect aktionsart by some kind of marked Imperfect. If there ever was such a drift, however, the   lexicialization went different ways in the branches of Chadic and would have to be attributed to the post-PC period.

In West Chadic—and the scattered evidence from East Chadic languages seems to support our claim for this branch too—a number of languages began to develop an innovative fourth verb stem to mark the aspectual notion of imperfective action in contrast to duration of state. This development became possible through redesignation (*réemploi de matériaux*) of verb stems with imperfective connotations whether from within or without the actual aktionsart system, i.e. the verbal noun and the plural verb stems. No matter from where the process originally started, the resulting verb formations eventually showed such an amount of structural similarity, much to the distress of comparative Chadicists, that one felt compelled to "reconstruct" an "imperfective stem" for the proto-language, i.e. a verb stem marked by infixation and/or suffixation of -*a* and possibly radical consonant gemination. "Imperfective stems" of such a shape did not only share common morphological features (internal and/or final *a*, doubling of final consonant) but also seemed to share common semantic features (habitual, continuous-progressive, future-intentional, etc.) which linguists usually associate with "imperfective aspect". Since, however, we have rejected the hypothesis that such an imperfective stem existed in PC, we now have to explain its development in those languages in which it does occur.

2.3.1.1 Imperfective Stem Development through Redesignation of Verbal Plurals

Radical consonant doubling (gemination) and/or insertion of *a* are well documented plural marking devices not only in Chadic but also in other families of Afroasiatic, and not only in the nominal but also in the verbal systems. As we have established in section 1.3 of this paper, verbal plurality encompasses the four related but distinct semantic areas of distributive, iterative, durative, and intensive. It is not difficult to imagine that verb plurals in toto were semantically limited to the durative and/or iterative nuances and that the same language or group of languages gave up the usage of plural verb stems to indicate distributive and intensive shades of meaning. We would expect such a language to have today a morphological opposition of non-imperfective/imperfective verb stems but to show no examples of verb plural stems. There may be other languages, in which iterative and/or durative on the one hand and distributive and/or intensive on the other hand became analyzed as reflecting two distinct categories of the language—imperfective ("inflexional") stems vs. "true" (derivational) plural stems—thereby splitting the original category of verbal plurality in two. In modern languages of this type we would expect productive plural verb stem formation. Both types represent "ideal types" or final stages of development. In praxis we would expect intermediate stages with fully developed imperfective stems and more or less restricted occurrence of plural stems. Under no circumstances would we, however, expect to find BOTH imperfectivity and plurality to be expressed in one and the same verb formation. In fact, this is the case in some modern Chadic languages which neutralize the non-plural/plural contrast in imperfective stem formations (cf. Wolff 1977b). In the closely related Ron group of West Chadic languages and the East Chadic language Migama verb plural stems are very restricted, i.e. limited to only a few verbs (only 5 in, for instance, Ron Sha (Jungraithmayr 1970:268)) and/or "lexicalized" as a phonological class of verb bases without semantic contrast (as possibly in Migama (Wolff 1977a). Note the following few examples for illustration:

	simple lexical base/stem	plural base/stem	imperfective stem	gloss
Migama	*ti-*		*tee-wa*	'eat'
	mat-	*matt-*		'die'
	lipid̃-		*lepedd̃-a*	'mould'
Ron-Sha	*gol*	*golol*		'break'
	bol		*bolôl*	'come'
	shish	*shaash*		'slaughter'
-Daffo	*shit*		*shyaät*	'look'
	ɓil	*ɓyal*		'draw water'
-Bokkos	*lul*		*lwaal*	'ask'

2.3.1.2 Imperfective Stem Development through Redesignation of Verbal Nouns

Another possibility which might account for the development of characteristically marked imperfective stems is to assume that true nouns which are etymologically related to verbs ("deverbative nouns" = DVN) were allowed to be substituted for verbal nouns in the periphrastic constructions which served to indicate Continuous et al. aktionsarten in PC. Such a substitution of verbal nouns by deverbative nouns was observed by Schuh (1976) in a number of West Chadic languages:

e.g.   Hausa   *ká-nàa sàyáa*   (VN)   'you(sg) are buying'
                   ká-nàa sàyée   (DVN)

       Ngizim   *k-àa d̃ánká-w*   (VN)   'you(sg) are sewing'
                   k-àa d̃ánák   (DVN)

       Karekare   *k-áa d̃áaƙaâ*   (VN)   'you(sg) are following'
                   k-áa d̃áaƙú yî (DVN)

Through such a development, I can imagine the actual verbal noun to loose more and more of its verbo-nominal nature and become reanalyzed as a fourth verb stem within the stem system of the particular language or language group.

Over time, vowel and consonant assimilations working regressively from the suffix *-wa* of the PC VN may affect the phonological shape of the verbal noun to such an extent that it can hardly be told apart at first sight from plural verb forms which are found elsewhere in Chadic (or even within the same language?). Hence, the attempt of comparative Chadicists to relate stems which are marked by "infixation and/or suffixation of *a*" to the same historical source. The confusion was brought about by the accidental fact that both verb plurals as well as verbal nouns made use of a formative containing the vowel *a*.

Both developments, innovation of an imperfective stem through redesignation of verbal plurals and of verbal nouns, can be graphically represented by Figures 11 and 12 respective

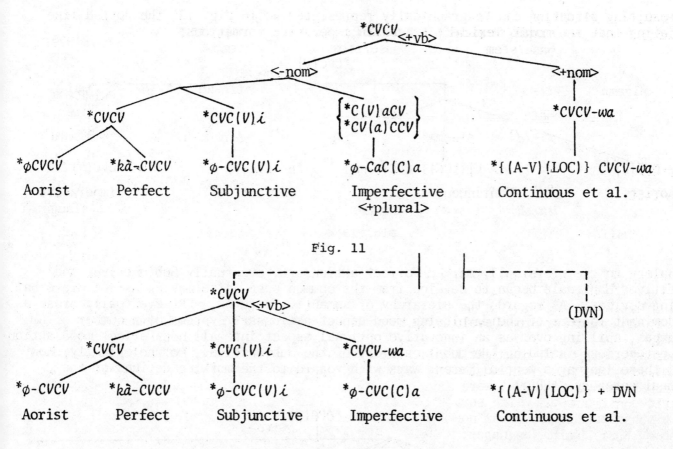

Fig. 11

Fig. 12

Accepting these two independent developments as plausible historical changes we can explain the existence of a fourth verb stem in a number of Chadic languages without being forced to reconstruct an imperfective stem for Proto-Chadic.

2.3.2 The Emergence of the Perfective in Biu-Mandara

One of the major differences between the P-BM dialect cluster and the rest of PC was the way in which the inherited aktionsart system developed. Whereas some non-BM proto-dialects elaborated the system further in a straightforward manner by developing an innovative fourth stem, i.e. the Imperfective stem in addition to the already existing lexical, modal, and verbal noun stems, many P-BM dialects seem to have undergone a serious breakdown of the morphological side of the system before innovative elaboration began in this branch too.

The morphological breakdown of the inherited system in P-BM dialects can be attributed to the almost complete loss of most if not all stem-final distinctions (the dialects differed in the extend to which they were affected by this apocopational tendency), i.e. the lexical, modal, and the verbo-nominal stems began to loose their segmentally contrastive features. (Whether this process was facilitated by the fact that suprasegmental marking had begun to accompany the segmental devices, cannot yet be established because the reverse process is also possible, namely that suprasegmental marking devices were developed in BM in compensation to the loosing of the segmental markers.) However, the lexical, modal, and verbo-nominal stems tended to become identical in shape, and syntactical means may have been the only devices by which some AUX-categories continued to be distinguished from each other, such as periphrasis, position of subject pronouns, etc.

The resulting situation can be graphically represented as in Fig. 13, the dotted line indicating that the modal stem left traces in imperative formations:

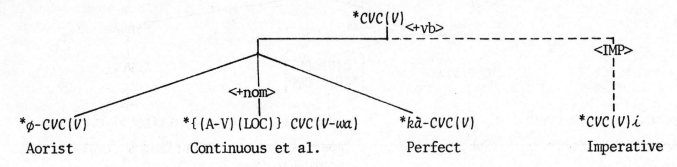

Fig. 13

By analogy to the preverbally marked Perfect aktionsart, eventually Subjunctives and Repetitives/Habituals began to develop from the common base, also making use of preverbal marking devices. As regards the hierarchy of semantic features, +PRF eventually arose as the dominant feature of the developing mood-aspect-aktionsart systems of a number of BM languages, spilling over as an innovative optional aspect into all non-Perfect mood/aktion- sart categories, including the modal category of the Subjunctive. Morphologically, how- ever, these languages went different ways with regard to the marking devices of the optional category <+PRF>:

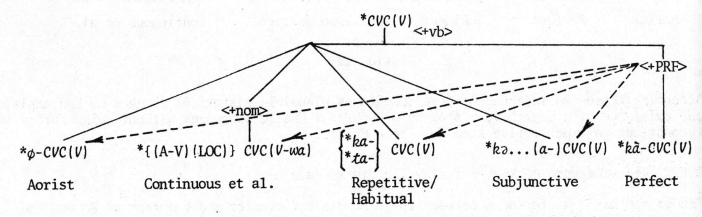

Fig. 19

3. SUMMARY AND CONCLUSIONS CONCERNING THE
"TENTATIVE FOUR STAGE MODEL FOR THE DEVELOPMENT OF THE CHADIC LANGUAGES"

I have attempted to demonstrate in this paper that no more than three verbal stems can and need be reconstructed for Proto-Chadic, on which the mood-aktionsart-system was built:

1. the "lexical" stem which displayed vowel-tone-classes
2. the "modal" stem which was marked by a termination $*i$
3. the "verbo-nominal" stem which was marked by a suffix $*-wa$

In the verb system, the lexical stem was used without any further marking devices to indica the indicative aktionsart "aorist". In combination with the preverbal marker $*ka$ this stem served to indicate the indicative aktionsart "perfect". The modal stem was used to form the "subjunctive" and "imperative" mood. The verbo-nominal stem was used in periphrastic construction, the "continuous-durative" being definitely among the so marked aktionsarten.

No "aspect stem" to mark the category of Imperfective as conceived of by Jungraithmayr and Schuh needs to be reconstructed for the proto-language. Verb stems in modern Chadic languages which are characteristically marked by internal -a- and/or -a suffix and/or gemination of final consonants, which are used for the formation of aktionsarten with imperfective connotations, are explained as being innovative redesignations of either plural verb stems or the proto-VN stem. Thus, the development of dichotomous aspect systems in a number of modern Chadic languages in which Imperfective is analyzed as a marked category is described as being a fairly recent innovation. Likewise innovative is the emergence of Perfective as a marked aspectual category in the verbal systems of languages of the Biu-Mandara branch.

For the time being, no suprasegmental marking devices are reconstructed for the Proto-Chadic verbal system. If tone played any role at all in the verbal system of the proto-language, it may have been strictly lexical or phonologically conditioned. At some later stage in the linguistic history of Chadic, tone began to play a grammatical role, at least in the verb systems of some Proto-Biu-Mandara dialects: one of the suggested working hypotheses assumes that Hi tone pattern on the verbal complex (= subject pronoun + verb stem) could be used to mark off derived categories of either aktionsart or time reference (tempus).

With regard to current theories on the nature and history of the Chadic verbal system, the comparative evidence presented in this paper suggests a departure from a number of claims traditionally held. This concerns, most of all, a theory developed by H. Jungraithmayr which became known as the "Tentative Four Stage Model for the Development of the Chadic Languages" (cf. section 1.4 of this paper). The generally accepted notion that Chadic has inherited a fundamental binary distinction of "aspect" in which a "Perfective" is unmarked and an "Imperfective" is marked, may now be questioned for several reasons. First of all, neither the Perfect (aktionsart) nor the Perfective (aspect) where it occurs in modern Chadic languages, can be accepted as having ever been unmarked, either semantically or morphologically, in the verb system at any stage in the linguistic history of Chadic. Rather, a third category must be set up as representing the unmarked category in the proto-language: In terms of aktionsarten we have suggested to label this unmarked category "aorist" (following another long established usage). Should for some reason this unmarked category need to be referred to in terms of aspects, the use of the label "Grundaspekt" as introduced by Jungraithmayr is suggested. Since the characteristically marked "imperfective stem" on which theories have been built cannot be reconstructed as such for Proto-Chadic, aspect systems where they do occur in modern languages of the family cannot be accepted as being retentions from Proto-Afroasiatic, despite surface similarities. If, however, we reinterpret the basic binary distinction between two sets of aktionsarten as relating to the truly verbal vs. verbo-nominal nature of the stems involved, then the term aspect is misleading and inappropriately applied to this syntactic dichotomy, since "aspect" ought to be reserved to relate to semantic distinctions. The generally accepted idea among Chadicists includes furthermore, that even though Chadic languages tend to have more than two or three verb moods/aktionsarten/aspects, all of these are reducible to two or three basic formations. We now propose that this idea relates morphologically and syntactically to the three distinct verb stems reconstructed above for the proto-language, and that, furthermore, a basic binary semantic distinction, which even today operates the verbal systems of a number of Chadic languages, is reconstructible for Proto-Chadic. This SEMANTIC dichotomy, however, may have had in the proto-language nothing to do with "aspect" but rather was related to the feature "plural" (in the widest sense) somewhere in the sentence. The analysis of the Proto-Chadic verbal system as presented in this paper does not exclude, in fact it stresses the likelihood of, the development of aspect systems, i.e. the development of di- or trichotomous systems in modern Chadic languages in which imperfective and/or perfective CONNOTATIONS of conjugational paradigms are accompanied by recurring morphological features in the verb stems involved. Thus, contrary to previous assumptions the notion of aspect does not appear to be adequate to classify aktionsarten at the level of the parent language. If, however, we insist on classifying these at a higher analytical level, then we should do so (i) syntactically on the basis of the feature <⁺nominal>, (ii) semantically on the basis of the feature <±plural>. In MODERN Chadic languages, however, a number of aktionsarten of a given language may indeed share semantic as well as morphological features in such a way that for synchronic descriptive purposes we may indeed be justified in classifying aktionsarten according to which "aspectual" set they belong to.

From a historical point of view, the "Four Stage Model" appears to be formulated upside down: HJ favors the idea that the historical development of the Chadic languages could be illustrated by proposing four (actually five: the fifth stage envisaged to account for the situation in Hausa) stages or steps in which the (Proto-Chadic) imperfective stem marking devices became more and more reduced and thus led to a simpler morphology of the stem in each stage.[18] Jungraithmayr's "simplification model" will be quoted below in the left column. Terms from the competing "elaboration model" as developed and presented in this paper are given in the right column to ensure comparability (they do not, of course, imply successive stages of development other than that "Proto-Chadic" represents the starting point for various developments):

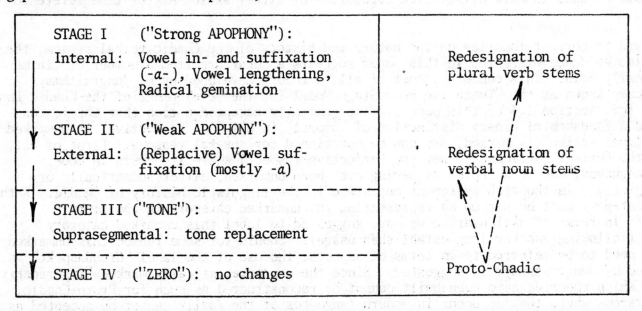

The theory of the multiple source for modern Chadic imperfective verb stems which is propose in this paper has immediate repercussions on the methodology of comparative Chadic verb morphology: the comparison of isolated verb forms in different languages will very likely not yield historically correct hypotheses concerning the nature and development of the Chadic verbal system—it is the systems as such which have to be compared and reconstructed.

---

[18]Such a view agrees with a traditional conceptual prejudice in African linguistics according to which African languages generally are assumed to be in the process of simplify ing rather than elaborating their various sub-systems. Jungraithmayr (1968c:19) explicitly admits this when he says that

> "From a methodological point of view we hold that the only possible
> direction of development as regards the history of these three dif-
> ferent behavioural patterns of the Verb Stem is one that runs from
> diversity to simplification."

As concerns the identification of the historical source of a given language's imperfective verb stem we must not only know what the verbal noun looks like in this language, but also whether verbal plurals occur—and if they occur, whether they co-occur with imperfective verb stems.

In concluding I wish to stress the fact that the ideas and hypotheses presented here are not supposed to serve as a watertight theory concerning origin and historical development of the modern Chadic mood-aspect-aktionsart systems. What I set out to do was to offer an alternative frame for the comparative study of Chadic verb morphology which in competition with previously proposed and widely accepted theories may serve to further our insights into a complex and fascinating subfield of Chadic linguistics.

REFERENCES

Carnochan, J. 1970. "Categories of the verbal piece in Bachama." *African Language Studies* 11:81-112.

Comrie, B. 1976. *Aspect. An Introduction to the Study of Verbal Aspect and Related Problems*. Cambridge: Cambridge University Press.

Dressler, W. 1968. *Studien zur Verbalen Pluralität. Iterativum, Distributivum, Durativum, Intensivum in der allgemeinen Grammatik, im Lateinischen und Hethitischen*. Wien.

Hoffmann, C. 1955. "Untersuchungen zur Struktur und sprachlichen Stellung des Bura." Ph.D. Dissertation, Hamburg.

Hoffmann, C. 1963. *A Grammar of the Margi Language*. London: Oxford University Press.

Jaouen, R. 1974. "Le verbe en giziga." Paper presented to the 11th West African Languages Congress at Yaounde, Cameroun, 1-5 April.

Jungraithmayr, H. 1966. "Zum Bau der Aspekte im Westtschadohamitischen." *ZDMG* 116:227-34.

Jungraithmayr, H. 1968a. "The Hamitosemitic Present-Habitative verb stem in Ron and Mubi." *Journal of West African Languages* 5:71-6.

Jungraithmayr, H. 1968b. "Ancient Hamito-Semitic Remnants in the Central Sudan." *African Language Review* 7:16-22.

Jungraithmayr, H. 1968c. "Hausa, Ron, Angas: a comparative analysis of their 'aspect' systems." *Afrika und Übersee* 52:15-22.

Jungraithmayr, H. 1970. *Die Ron-Sprachen. Tschadohamitische Studien in Nordnigerien*. Glückstadt: Verlag J.J. Augustin.

Jungraithmayr, H. 1975a. "Types of conjugational forms in Chadic." In J. Bynon and T. Bynon (eds.), *Hamito-Semitica*, pp. 399-413. The Hague: Mouton.

Jungraithmayr, H. 1975b. "Der Imperfektivstamm im Migama." *Folia Orientalia* 16:85-100.

Jungraithmayr, H. 1976. "Apophony and tone in the Afroasiatic/Niger-Congo frontier area." Paper presented to the 12th West African Languages Congress at Ife, Nigeria, 14-20 March.

Jungraithmayr, H. In press (a). "Apophony and grammatical tone in the tense system of Chadic languages." *Afrika und Übersee*.

Jungraithmayr, H.   In press (b).   "A tentative four stage model for the development of the Chadic languages."   *Proceedings of the second international congress on Hamito-Semitic linguistics*.   Florence.

Klingenheben, A.   1928/29.   "Die Tempora Westafrikas und die Semitischen Tempora."   *Zeitschrift für Eingeborenensprachen* 19:241-68.

Lukas, J.   1937.   *Die Logone-Sprache im Zentralen Sudan*.   (Auszug).   Bonn: Bonner Universitäts-Buchdruckerei Gebr. Scheur.

Lukas, J.   1970.   *Studien zur Sprache der Gisiga (Nordkamerun)*.   Glückstadt: Verlag J.J. Augustin.

Lyons, J.   1968.   *Introduction to Theoretical Linguistics*.   Cambridge: Cambridge University Press.

Meek, C.K.   1931.   *Tribal Studies in Northern Nigeria*. 2 vols.   London.

Meyer-Bahlburg, H.   1972.   *Studien zur Morphologie und Syntax des Musgu*.   Hamburg: Helmut Buske Verlag.

Mirt, H.   1971.   "Zur Morphologie des Verbalkomplexes im Mandara."   *Afrika und Übersee* 54:1-76.

Moscati, S., and A. Spitaler, E. Ullendorf, W.v. Soden. 1962^2.   *An Introduction to the Comparative Grammar of the Semitic Languages*.   Wiesbaden: Otto Harrassowitz.

Newman, P.   1970.   *A Grammar of Tera*.   Berkeley: University of California Press.

Newman, P.   1975.   "Proto-Chadic verb classes."   *Folia Orientalia* 16:65-84.

Newman, P.   1977a.   "The formation of the imperfective stem in Chadic."   *Afrika und Übersee* 60:178-92.

Newman, P.   1977b.   "Chadic classification and reconstructions."   *Afroasiatic Linguistics* 5(1):1-42.

Newman, P.   In press.   "Chado-Hamitic 'Adieu': new thoughts on Chadic language classification."   *Proceedings of the Second International Congress on Hamito-Semitic Linguistics*.   Florence.

Newman, P., and R. Ma.   1966.   "Comparative Chadic: phonology and lexicon."   *Journal of African Languages* 5:218-51.

Newman, P., and R.G. Schuh.   1974.   "The Hausa aspect system."   *Afroasiatic Linguistics* 1(1):1-39.

Newman, R. Ma.   1971.   "A case grammar of Ga'anda."   Ph.D. Dissertation, University of California, Los Angeles.

Ryder, Stuart A., II.   1974.   *The D-Stem in Western Semitic*.   The Hague: Mouton.

Schuh, R.G.   1976.   "The Chadic verbal system and its Afroasiatic nature."   *Afroasiatic Linguistics* 3(1):1-14.

Schuh, R.G.   1977.   "West Chadic verb classes."   In P. Newman and R.M. Newman (eds.), *Papers in Chadic Linguistics*, pp. 143-66.   Leiden: Afrika-Studiecentrum.

Smith, D.M.   1969.   "The Kapsiki language."   Ph.D. Dissertation, Michigan State University.

Wolff, E.   1972.   "Die Verbalphrase des Laamang."   Ph.D. Dissertation, Hamburg.

Wolff, E.   1977a.   "Verb bases and stems in Migama."   *Afrika und Übersee* 60:163-77.

Wolff, E.   1977b.   "Patterns in Chadic (and Afroasiatic?) verb base formations."   In P. Newman and R.M. Newman (eds.), *Papers in Chadic Linguistics*, pp. 199-233.   Leiden: Afrika-Studiecentrum.

Zaborski, A.   1975.   *The Verb in Cushitic*.   Warszawa-Kraków. Nakładem Uniwersytetu Jagiellóuskiego.